Race, Nation, War

This book examines international post-9/11 policies by connecting them to the US violations of Japanese Americans' human rights during World War II. Analysing the policies of the United States, *Race, Nation, War* illustrates how ideas of race and masculinity shaped the indefinite leave policy which the government used to move Japanese Americans out of camps during the war. With attention to recent American and European policies, the author demonstrates that race, gender, and nation also converge in President Trump's policies on refugees and human rights, the German and European migrant crises, and related German policies and politics. Assayed from a unique city and regional planning perspective, *Race, Nation, War* will appeal not only to scholars of planning, but also to those with interests in American Studies, gender studies, race and ethnicity, sociology, history, and public policy.

Ayanna Yonemura is a lecturer in the Ethnic Studies and Sociology Departments at California State University Sacramento, USA. Her research looks at race, public policy, and urban planning from a feminist perspective.

Race, Nation, War
Japanese American Forced Removal, Public Policy and National Security

Ayanna Yonemura

LONDON AND NEW YORK

First published 2019 by Routledge

2 Park Square, Milton Park, Abingdon, Oxon, OX14 4RN

605 Third Avenue, New York, NY 10017

Routledge is an imprint of the Taylor & Francis Group, an informa business

First issued in paperback 2020

British Library Cataloguing-in-Publication Data
A catalogue record for this book is available from the British Library

Library of Congress Cataloging-in-Publication Data
A catalog record has been requested for this book

ISBN: 978-1-138-60637-1 (hbk)
ISBN: 978-0-367-72769-7 (pbk)

Typeset in Times New Roman
by codeMantra

This book is dedicated to my father, Mitsugi Yonemura.

Contents

Figures

Acknowledgments

Trying to thank people who assisted and supported me in writing this book is a daunting task. The list of people to whom I am grateful is a long one, and there are the restraints of space to contend with as well as, no doubt, a limited memory as many aspects of the book originated a long time ago. I am very grateful to my parents for their consistent confidence in me and support of this project and endless others that I have undertaken. The friendships of Carla Cain, Tammi Monsanto, and William and Kit Chang have seen me through the highs and lows of graduate school and beyond.

An enormous thank you goes to Shirley Hune, my PhD advisor, without whom I would not have undertaken a historical topic for my dissertation. She was also my mentor for UCLA's Graduate Division's Summer Research Institute Fellowship, which allowed me to concentrate on policies that targeted Japanese Americans during World War II during my first summer as a doctoral student. It takes committees to raise doctoral students, and everyone on my committees shaped this book as well as who I am today. In addition to Shirley, they are Leobardo Estrada, Yuji Ichioka, Don Nakanishi, Abel Valenzuela, and Ed Soja.

Before and since my graduate years, many scholars have been very supportive. Lois Takahashi and Sondra Hale have provided me with years of intellectual advice and endless inspiration dating back to my M.A. student years, when I took a course from Sondra, and my immediate post-doctoral years, when I met Lois. Lois was one of the first to provide me direction on this project, and her insights have improved it enormously ever since. My undergraduate professors first nurtured my efforts to analyze race, gender, and nationalism. Some of the many wonderful faculty members at University of California at Santa Cruz who contributed to my intellectual growth are Bettina Aptheker and Angela Davis as well as Loisa Nygaard and John Brown Childs who advised me on my B.A. thesis. Dr. Ricky Green and the Interdisciplinary Faculty Community on Immigration, both of California State University Sacramento, provided generous feedback during the critical months before I completed the manuscript.

The institutions that have supported this book or the doctoral dissertation that is its foundation include UCLA's Institute of American Cultures, UCLA's Graduate Division and UCLA's Urban Planning Department. A Civil Liberties Public Education Fund National Fellowship funded my dissertation research. Grants from California State University Sacramento's College of Social Sciences and Interdisciplinary Studies also provided valued support.

1 Introduction

As a presidential candidate and as U.S. President, Donald Trump has routinely performed a type of masculinity which includes boasting about the size of his body parts and employing, what some commentators have called, "the language of domestic violence."[1] "Doing gender," to use the term which West and Zimmerman coined, Trump has enacted a plethora of "ideas of masculinity. . . so pervasive that they [have] become a natural way. . . to make policy."[2] The president also regularly articulates the hegemonic idea that European and European-derived cultures are, as Edward Said explains, "superior in comparison with all non-European peoples and cultures."[3] American notions of race and gender are "shaped by a uniquely American experience" as well as "[s]hared with other societies" and particularly with European societies and others founded by European settler colonists. Ronald Takaki's description of World War II policymakers applies to presidents and their advisors since World War II as well, ". . .they had grown up and were living in a culture that defined how men and women should behave."[4]

This book presents three moments in which ideologies of cultural superiority and gender manifested in national policies during times of war. They are the United States' World War II forced removal and incarceration of Japanese Americans; U.S. President Donald Trump's refugee policies during the so-called war on terror; and contemporary and parallel refugee policies in Germany under Chancellor Angela Merkel. I explore these moments through the lenses of cultural domination, gender ideology, and policymakers' intersecting cultural contexts especially those pertaining to race, class, and nationality.[5] Legal scholar Jerry Kang speaks to the significance of Japanese American history to national security policies in the post-9/11 era,

We are fighting an indefinite war on terror. In considering the policy and practice of this war, the history of Japanese American internment looms large. . . It is only through constant vigilance that the internment can remain a lighthouse that helps us navigate the rocky shores triangulated by freedom, equality, and security. We can never presume 'never again.'[6]

Far from being an aberration, Mr. Trump's ideologies are ubiquitous in European and Euro-American politics historically as well as in the twenty-first century.[7] This book responds to the ways in which ideas of race, gender, and nation converge during the so-called war on terror by connecting them to the United States' World War II policies on Japanese Americans.[8] By relating the World War II-era policies to U.S. and international post–September 11, 2001 policies, my aim is to shed light on the tenacious myth of white cultural superiority, its significance in the twenty-first century, and its entanglements with gender ideologies and national identities.

An interdisciplinary inquiry, this book relies on theories and methods from gender studies, postcolonial studies, ethnic studies, and history to analyze public policy, public administration, and politics. As it originated with a dissertation on the hidden history of urban and regional planning's influence on cultural domination in War Relocation Authority's (WRA) policy, this book is, partly, a history of urban and regional planning and the related disciplines of applied sociology and anthropology. While *Race, Nation, War* mostly concentrates on the U.S. and Japanese Americans, comparisons within and between the United States, global, and historical contexts are an indispensable strategy for demonstrating the continuity of the idea of white cultural superiority.

As Robert Dean describes in *Imperial Brotherhood: Gender and the Making of Cold War Foreign Policy*, this book "assumes that [policymakers] . . . are complex, socially constructed beings, who act from a repertoire of possibilities that are a product of their experience. . . [and that] policy reason, too, is thus culturally constructed and reproduced."[9] Analyzing policy includes understanding "the formative patterns of class and gender among the policymakers."[10] I incorporate intersectional analyses of class and gender along with race and nation to unravel policy epistemology and why particular policymakers considered certain policies possible and desirable.[11]

Like other cultural constructs, masculinity and femininity ideologies vary as do gender performances and ways of doing gender. West and Zimmerman point out that "The meanings people attach to particular gender-, race-, or class-appropriate conduct come from historically specific institutional and collective practices in the . . . allocation of material and symbolic resources."[12] Public policy allocates "material and symbolic resources" on the basis of "institutional and collective practices" and is often a way of doing gender.[13]

This book utilizes primary sources including public documents, correspondence, policy statements, Congressional testimonies, and speeches accessed via the U.S. National Archives, the Truman Library in Independence, Missouri, and Special Collections at the University of California Los Angeles and the University of Arizona in Tucson. It also incorporates reinterpretations of secondary studies and interpretations of biographies and autobiographies. Reports from organizations such as the Southern Poverty Law Center and the United Nations provide information on recent events including German and U.S. elections, migration data, and policy debates.

This book's focus on the United States and Germany reflects those nations' relevance to the topic of nationalism and war as well as my personal and scholarly relationships with the United States and Germany. One could conduct parallel analyses of other European and European-derived nations. France and Australia come to mind. This book, though, is about the two countries with which I am most familiar.

As a world power since 1898 and a twenty-first-century global super power, the United States is a singularly influential nation. It also purports to be the world's largest democracy yet suffers from a racist present and past. A nation built with enslaved labor on colonized land, the United States has the world's largest economy and third largest population with growth primarily fueled by immigration from Latin America and Asia. Demographers predict that by 2050, whites will no longer be a majority, but if inequalities persist, the United States will resemble Brazil or South Africa where wealth and resources are concentrated in a white minority.[14]

Germany is the European Union's most populous and economically powerful member. According to global studies professor Joyce Marie Mushaben, the recruitment of skilled workers, the need for a tax base to support the aging population, postunification cultural changes, and a "new human rights" culture has led to a German "paradigm shift in citizenship and migration policies."[15] Since the fall of the Berlin Wall in 1989, Germany has gone from a country that rejected immigration to one with a "welcoming culture." Before that change, though, Chancellor Helmut Kohl's government tightened migration and refugee policies. During his chancellorship and shortly after unification, the nation experienced the racist violence of 1991–1993 which included multiple fire-bombings of housing for people seeking asylum. My earliest reflections about racism, nationalism, and policy were during the time of this historic violence when I researched and wrote an undergraduate thesis on Germany's political asylum policy. The racist nationalism of those years complicated the plights of people seeking refuge in a country where neither the policies nor much of the population were welcoming.[16]

With the 1999 Citizenship and Naturalization Law, Germany broke with laws which dated back to 1913 and defined citizenship by *jus sanguinis* ("law of blood"). Mushaben writes that Chancellor Merkel has accomplished "more to advance the legal rights and day-to-day opportunities of foreigners and their offspring than all of her predecessors' reforms dating back to 1949."[17]

Cultural domination

At the time of writing, nationalist narratives that portray refugees as threatening, inferior people are increasingly manifesting in German and U.S. policies. As George Lipsitz writes, "The possessive investment in whiteness fuels depictions of aggrieved racialized populations as innately risky, as unworthy of protection or support. . ."[18] Regardless of national and international laws designed to protect them, depictions of the type which Lipsitz describes contribute to the criminalization of refugees. Ideals pertaining to "rights," whether described as "human," "civil" or both, are fundamental to U.S. and European identities and narratives which position these nations as superior to non-Euro-American nations. Paradoxically, the crises of refugee politics have exposed the racism and ideas of cultural domination which are integral to these North American and European countries.[19]

In *Orientalism*, Edward Said argues that the ideology of white cultural superiority is fundamental to maintaining Europe and the United States' power on the global stage. Said points out that ". . . the major component in European culture is precisely what made that culture hegemonic both in and outside Europe: the idea of European identity as a superior one in comparison with all the non-European peoples and cultures."[20] This idea connects racism against refugees with that perpetrated against nonwhites within their own countries. The influence of Western cultural domination is not limited to Europe, the United States, and "the Orient." Globally, it is part and parcel to the ongoing hierarchical relationships between and within regions, nations, and peoples.[21]

It is necessary to understand cultural domination in order to fully understand Europe and the United States' economic and political power as well as the disproportionate power of whiteness and white people. This domination accounts for the ability to subject people to hate crimes and homelessness as well as to reject people even when that means exposing them to the horrors of human trafficking, sexual assault, and death by drowning in the Mediterranean or of thirst in North American deserts. Following Said's lead, this book is concerned with, ". . . Western conceptions and treatments of the Other but also with the singularly important role played by Western culture in . . . the world of nations."[22] Ronald Takaki and Alexander Saxton, who have dissected the idea of white cultural superiority's "cultural leadership," are significant inspirations.[23]

Said, Takaki, and Saxton are part of a post-Gramscian approach. Said summarizes Antonio Gramsci's use of hegemony: "In any society . . . certain ideas are more influential than others; the form of this cultural leadership is what Gramsci has identified as *hegemony.* . ."[24] Human rights-related policies, whether part of discourse on "refugee policy," "racism," "civil rights," or "civil liberties," go to the heart of the cultural leadership of the idea of white cultural superiority. In international relations, European and U.S. discourses on "democracy," "freedom," and "equality" often serve as proxies for claims which contrast "Western civilization" with nonwhites supposedly savage, heathen, or backward ways.[25]

Paradoxically, in juxtaposition to these claims, Western global dominance of the last several centuries has been based on the exploitation of nonwhite peoples and non-European places. The ongoing cultural hegemony and political, economic, and military dominance rest on such undemocratic and inhumane forms of oppression as colonialism and enslavement.[26] While the West does not have a monopoly on oppression or paradoxes, Western and white actions and ideas are the pillars of Western domination and, therefore, the focus of this book.

Said, Takaki, and Saxton's studies of dominant culture encompass large scopes of geography, racialized groups, and historical eras. The results are comparisons that produce comprehensive understandings of the idea of Euro-American superiority, its continuity, and how it supports Euro-American domination. For example, Takaki's comparative analysis of different U.S. racialized groups within the context of class divisions demonstrates the interconnectedness of groups' experiences and allows him to study American society and culture as a "total structure."[27] While *Race, Nation, War*'s scope is modest, comparisons of historical eras, populations, and nations are intended to demonstrate the continuity of the idea Euro-American cultural superiority as well as the specificities of how it plays out with particular actors and in particular times and places.

U.S. nationalism, along with that of many, if not all, European countries, incorporates a fusion of racism, patriarchy, and class dimensions, which creates a myth of exceptionalism. By the nineteenth century, the United States had created a national identity according to which it was distinct from, and superior to, Europe. Nonetheless, European ideas of race, whiteness, and cultural superiority permeate modern U.S. national identity and those of European nations. Susan-Mary Grant, Professor of American History at Newcastle University, explains that the U.S. national origin myth centers on the Revolutionary War "as an expression of universal rights."[28] White men, the elite so-called founding fathers, feature almost exclusively in this myth, which feeds a white, patriarchal national identity.[29]

In the 2016 U.S. election and the German elections of 2017 and 2018, nationalist politicians played to, what Lipsitz terms, whites' "fantasies of uninhibited power" and feelings of being "grievously victimized."[30] The results were Donald Trump's election to the U.S. presidency and Chancellor Merkel's losses to the anti-immigration Alternative Party for Deutschland (AfD). Mr. Trump and the AfD leaders are exam-ples of politicians whose success depends on racist national identities, their white compatriots' feelings of entitlement, and manipulating the so-called war on terror to support their agendas. Their victories have patriarchal overtones. In Germany and in the United States, racist politicians position themselves as heroes protecting white women and girls from refugees and immigrants whom they portray as brown and black hordes of sexual predators.[31]

It is a fallacy, though, to attribute this electoral trend exclusively to the recent surge in nationalism. In "White Nationalism, Armed Culture and State Violence in the Age of Donald Trump," Henry A. Giroux points out liberals' and Democrats' hypocrisy:

> In the face of Trump's unapologetic authoritarianism, Dem-ocratic Party members and the liberal elite are trying to place themselves in the forefront of organized resistance. . . It is dif-ficult not to see such moral outrage and resistance as hypocriti-cal in light of the role they have played in the last forty years of subverting democracy and throwing minorities of class and color under the bus.[32]

In noting liberal hypocrisy in the Trump era, Giroux directs our atten-tion to liberals' participation in "undoing the social contract and the democratic, political and personal freedoms gained in the New Deal [which] culminat[ed] in the civil rights and educational struggles of the 1960s."[33] Liberals built the New Deal in the 1930s and a later genera-tion of liberals participated in "undoing" its social contract.

Dillon Myer was one of thousands of civil servants who built their careers in New Deal programs. He applied his New Deal mentality to Japanese Americans as, in 1942, President Roosevelt appointed Myer director of the WRA. The WRA was the federal agency charged with "supervising" Japanese Americans whom the government had removed from the West Coast and incarcerated in concentration camps.[34] As Orin Starn writes in his analysis of anthropology and the WRA,

> Representations of removal as progress meshed perfectly with broader New Deal and wartime semiotics of America rising out of the Depression with brawn, industry, and technology, and fed the WRA's aspiration of contributing—along with the WPA [Works Progress Administration], CWA [Civil Works Administration], TVA [Tennessee Valley Authority] and other great 1930s agencies whose name it invoked—to the massive project of national reconstruction.[35]

Like the Orientalists whom Said studies, Myer and his WRA team implemented a project of domination, and the idea of white cultural superiority was a basic premise of their professional culture.

Gender ideologies

The professionals who worked for the WRA incorporated patriarchal as well as racial backgrounds into their professional cultures. Their assimilationist approach was influenced by science and social science, which they identified as male-centered, rational, and intelligent. As Warwick Anderson describes white male health officers in the U.S.-occupied Philippines, the overwhelmingly male WRA staff subscribed to a masculinity ideology, which included, "see[ing] themselves as progressive and pragmatic representatives of modern American science . . ."[36] As much as this book is a study of cultural domination, it is also a study of gender ideologies as the two are intimately entangled.

Feminist scholars paved the way for studying gender ideologies, and in the last 20 plus years, scholars have developed masculinity studies to better understand how ideas of masculinity have impacted cultures as well as people of all genders and various class stratum. Joan Scott argues that "gender is a primary way of signifying relationships of power . . . politics construct gender, and gender constructs politics."[37] In *Hiroshima: Why America Dropped the Atomic Bomb*, Takaki examines the political elite at the end of World War II whom he describes as the "white men in positions of influence and power." He determines how ingrained ideas of gender contributed to the decision to drop the atomic bomb and played an important role in President Truman's international negotiations.[38]

Takaki applies C. Wright Mills' "sociological imagination" to analyze the "intersection between biography and history within society."[39] He especially focuses on President Truman who was ultimately responsible for the decision to drop the atomic bomb. Following this example, I employ the "sociological imagination" to analyze the WRA director, Myer, who was the chief architect of the WRA's policies.

Dean argues that "Ideals of 'manhood' or 'womanhood' held by society. . . are circulated throughout the culture and . . . individually internalized." He continues by explaining that an ideology of masculinity is ". . . a subset of a larger 'gender discourse'—a symbolic system of meaning by which social relations of power and privilege are rendered 'natural' and transparent. . ."[40] He applies the term "ideology of masculinity" to interpret the "Imperial Brotherhood," which he explains as the "establishment" which dominated U.S. foreign policy between 1947 and 1968.

Although Dean connects the Imperial Brotherhood to the Cold War, the concept is also helpful for identifying masculinity ideology during World War II. Lending credence to its World War II-era application, the Imperial Brotherhood reflected a Stimsonian ideal. The Brothers admired World War II Secretary of War Henry L. Stimson (1867–1950) for his stoicism, heroism, toughness, optimism, resoluteness, intelligence, and "manly spirit" of restraint. They also participated in his imperialist vision.[41]

Dean describes the Imperial Brotherhood's composition of "men who shared strikingly similar patterns of educational, social, and, in many cases, class background." He includes John F. Kennedy, Lyndon B. Johnson, John J. McCloy, and Robert McNamara in its membership. U.S. president from 1936 until he died in 1945, Franklin D. Roosevelt also fits the Imperial Brother typology. He shared the Brothers' upper-class ". . . institutions [boarding schools, Ivy League fraternities, elite military service, clubs which] . . . imbue[d] men with a particular kind of 'manhood'" and ingrained in them "an indoctrination in an 'ideology of masculinity' and the ritual creation of a fictive brotherhood of privilege and power."[42]

Applying "Imperial Brotherhood" along with the concept, "Bourgeois Brotherhood," allows me to interpret the men of middle-class origin whom Dean places in the Imperial Brotherhood. President Truman, who as then-Vice President succeeded Mr. Roosevelt in 1945, fits the Bourgeois Brother typology. The Bourgeois Brothers shared gendered and national values with the Imperials and operated with them at the highest level of U.S. government, but their class and geographic origins were different. The Bourgeois Brothers were born in small towns and rural areas. They worked their way up in status and migrated to Washington, D.C. through regional old boys' networks, which middle-class white men operationalized as a *de facto* affirmative action program for each other and themselves.

Dillon Myer was also a Bourgeois Brother. Having moved to Washington, D.C. with the help of a Midwestern old boys' network, Myer enjoyed his first Presidential appointment and entered the Bourgeois Brotherhood as WRA director. In order to understand how cultural domination played out in WRA policy, it is necessary to understand middle-class, patriarchal culture and masculinity ideology as well as the elite Brotherhoods' masculinity ideology, which guided how elected politicians, Presidential appointees, and cabinet members formulated policy.

Book structure

Chapter 2 orients the reader to World War II-era policy as it related to Japanese Americans' human rights violations and, especially, the WRA's indefinite leave policy. My aim is to provide the background for Chapters 3 and 4 particularly for readers less familiar with this history. Most Japanese Americans remained imprisoned throughout the war but, during the war, the WRA dispersed a third of its camps' population into the Midwest and East Coast. The WRA implemented this "scattering," as Richard Drinnon calls it, via the indefinite leave policy, which was one of the agency's top priorities.[43] Indefinite leave was the WRA's main method for its assimilationist agenda and, therefore, it provides a window into the contemporary theories on race and how policymakers implemented them. It directly impacted the 35,000 people who, based on it, were released from the camps, those Japanese Americans whose indefinite leave applications were not approved as well as those who, out of fear of poverty and racism, did not want indefinite leave and endured the WRA's attempts to coerce them into it.

Chapter 3 employs the "sociological imagination" to study how masculinity ideologies shaped WRA policies.[44] I examine the intersection between the WRA and Myer. As a Presidential appointee, Myer joined the Bourgeois Brotherhood, a group of men with middle-class origins who, along with elite-born men, dominated U.S. politics and whose gender, race, national, and cultural backgrounds manifested in policy. The Brotherhood and Myer's old boys' network demonstrate the patriarchy which was intrinsic to the New Deal and to the World War II-era U.S. government.

Myer shared a masculinity ideology with other policymakers. This ideology intersected with assimilation theories, the idea of white cultural superiority, and wartime propaganda. In policies, politics, and propaganda, Myer reinscribed war's centrality to masculinity, enforced Euro-American cultural dominance and utilized Japanese American soldiers to support his WRA narrative. While he never participated in war's physical aggression, Myer advocated for releasing Japanese American men from WRA camps to serve in the military. He employed Japanese American soldiers' sacrifices in strategies aimed at assimilating Japanese Americans, compelling white Americans to recognize Japanese American assimilation and convincing international onlookers of the United States' cultural superiority over the Axis powers.

Chapter 4 reveals a hidden history of city and regional planning and the WRA. City and regional planning and other social sciences shaped WRA policy and its assimilation agenda. In the United States, the 1940s was a turning point in hegemonic conceptions of race. While conservatives still believed that culture and ancestry were irretrievably linked, liberals valued assimilation and argued that culture was independent from ancestry. Because they accepted the myth of white cultural superiority, for liberals, assimilation was a unidirectional process, which improved nonwhites and left whites unchanged.

For Myer and his staff, Japanese Americans' indefinite leave out of the camps and into the East Coast and Midwest exemplified "the American way" of dealing with a "race problem." In contradistinction to domestic conservatives and the Axis powers, the WRA built on the New Deal legacy of applying city and regional planning (planning), sociology, and anthropology to nonwhites and was part of planning's social reform tradition. The United States' World War II violations of Japanese Americans' human rights was a moment in which liberals partook in white domination, disrupted and entrenched dominant notions of national identity, and contributed to the myth of white cultural superiority.

Chapter 5 explores the ideology of white cultural superiority and gender ideologies in the twenty-first century. Cultural contexts and ideas of white cultural superiority reflect the human dimensions of twenty-first-century political leaders as they did those of leaders during World War II. Dillon Myer directed the WRA during World War II—a significant turning point in white supremacist ideology when National Socialists discredited the then-dominant notion of innate white superiority. While Myer rejected the idea of white physical superiority, he enforced white cultural superiority, which remains a powerful facet of Euro-American domination in the twenty-first century. U.S. President Donald Trump and German Chancellor Angela Merkel and the controversies surrounding their refugee policies serve as opportunities to investigate twenty-first-century manifestations of gender ideologies and the ideology of white cultural superiority.

Notes

1 BBC News, "Trump to Kim: My Nuclear Button Is 'Bigger and More Powerful,'" Jan. 3, 2018, www.bbc.com/news/world-asia-42549687. Saba Hamedy and Joyce Tseng, "All the Times President Trump Has Insulted North Korea," *CNN*, March 9, 2018, www.cnn.com/2017/09/22/politics/donald-trump-north-korea-insults-timeline/index.html. Jessica Winter, "The Language of the Trump Administration Is the Language of Domestic Violence," *New Yorker*, June 11, 2018, www.newyorker.com/culture/cultural-comment/the-language-of-the-trump-administration-is-the-language-of-domestic-violence.
2 Candace West and Don H. Zimmerman, "Accounting for Doing Gender," *Gender & Society* 23, no. 1 (Feb. 2009): 112. Ronald T. Takaki, *Hiroshima: Why America Dropped the Atomic Bomb* (Boston, MA: Little, Brown, and Co., 1995).
3 Crispin Sartwell, "All the President's Men and Their Styles of Masculinity; Trump Be the First Man with His Particular Sort of Swagger to Make It to the White House," *Wall Street Journal* (Online), Aug. 4, 2017, http://proxy.lib.csus.edu/login?url=https://search-proquest-com.proxy.lib.csus.edu/docview/1925905705?accountid=10358. David A. Fahrenthold, "Trump Recorded Having Extremely Lewd Conversation about Women in 2005," Oct. 8, 2016, www.washingtonpost.com/politics/trump-recorded-having-extremely-lewd-conversation-about-women-in-2005/2016/10/07/3b9ce776-8cb4-11e6-bf8a-3d26847eeed4_story.html?utm_term=.55fee45a88c4. Edward W. Said, *Orientalism*, 1st ed. (New York: Pantheon Books, 1978), 7.
4 Takaki, *Hiroshima*, 115.
5 Robert Connell, *Masculinities* (Berkeley, CA: University of California Press, 2005), 75. Connell explains that gender is a way of structuring social practice and, therefore, unavoidably involved with other social structures including race, class and nationality.
6 Jerry Kang, "Watching the Watchers: Enemy Combatants in the Internment's Shadow," *Law and Contemporary Problems* 68, no. 2 (2005): 255, 280, https://scholarship.law.duke.edu/lcp/vol68/iss2/.
7 Aaron Belkin, *Bring Me Men: Military Masculinity and the Benign Façade of American Empire, 1898–2001* (New York: Columbia University Press, 2012), 2–3. Robert D. Dean, *Imperial Brotherhood: Gender and the Making of Cold War Foreign Policy* (Amherst: University of Massachusetts, 2003), 3–4, 50, 52, 169. www.washingtonpost.com/politics/trump-recorded-having-extremely-lewd-conversation-about-women-in-

2005/2016/10/07/3b9ce776-8cb4-11e6-bf8a-3d26847eeed4_story.html?utm_
term=.b28dcf5d9218. George Lipsitz, *The Possessive Investment in
Whiteness: How White People Profit from Identity Politics* (Philadelphia,
PA: Temple University Press, 2018), 83, ProQuest Ebook Central, https://
ebookcentral.proquest.com/lib/csus/detail.action?docID=542533483.
8 Henceforth, in referring to Japanese nationals residing in the United
States and U.S. citizens of Japanese heritage, I will use the term "Japanese
Americans."
9 Dean, 3.
10 Ibid.
11 See Brenda M. Boyle, *Masculinity in Vietnam War Narratives: A Critical
Study of Fiction, Films and Nonfiction Writings* (Jefferson, NC: McFarland &
Company, 2009), 64, cited in Belkin, 31.
12 West and Zimmerman, 115. Sarah Fenstermaker and Candace West,
"'Doing Difference' Revisited: Problems, Prospects, and the Dialogue
in Feminist Theory," in *Doing Gender: Doing Difference*, ed. Sarah
Fenstermaker and Candace West (New York: Routledge, 2002), 213,
quoted in West and Zimmerman, 115.
13 Ibid.
14 President Bill Clinton's address to the 1997 graduating class of the University of California at San Diego, quoted in Ronald Takaki, *A Different
Mirror: A History of Multicultural America* (New York: Back Bay Books,
2018), 434–435.
15 Joyce Marie Mushaben, *Becoming Madam Chancellor: Angela Merkel and
the Berlin Republic* (Cambridge: Cambridge University Press, 2017), 255.
16 Ibid., 253–254.
17 Ibid., 250, 255.
18 Lipsitz, xxvii.
19 UNHCR, "A Guide to International Refugee Protection and Building State Asylum Systems," 2017, www.unhcr.org/en-us/publications/
legal/3d4aba564/refugee-protection-guide-international-refugee-law-
handbook-parliamentarians.html?query=refugee%20law. Henceforth,
except in cases in which I specify otherwise, I will use "refugees" to refer
to those with refugee status as well as people seeking political asylum.
For UN definitions, see "Refugee," International Migration Glossary,
UNESCO, 2017, www.unesco.org/new/en/social-and-human-sciences/
themes/international-migration/glossary/refugee. And "Asylum Seeker,"
International Migration Glossary, UNESCO, 2017, www.unesco.org/new/
en/social-and-human-sciences/themes/international-migration/glossary/
asylum-seeker/.
20 Said, 7.
21 Ibid.
22 Lipsitz, xxvii. Said, 3–4, 24–25.
23 Ronald Takaki, *Iron Cages: Race and Culture in Nineteenth-Century
America*, 1st ed. (New York: Alfred A. Knopf, 1979). Alexander Saxton,
*The Rise and Fall of the White Republic: Class Politics and Mass Culture in
Nineteenth-Century America* (London: Verso, 1990). Said, 7.
24 Said, 7.
25 Ibid., 1–2, 7. In historical and twenty-first century European and Western
narratives, defining what the West is not is part of defining the West.

As Said explains, "the Orient has helped to define Europe (or the West) as its contrasting image, idea, personality, experience" and "There is in addition the hegemony of European ideas about the Orient, themselves reiterating European superiority over Oriental backwardness...."

26 James Walvin, "Symbols of Moral Superiority," in *Manliness and Morality: Middle-Class Masculinity in Britain and America, 1800–1940*, ed. J.A. Mangan and James Walvin (Manchester: Manchester University Press, 1987), 244. Such twenty-first century contradictions have historical precedents. Walvin explains that, after abolition, British anti-slavery activists considered,

> Slavery, along with 'heathenism,'... as a major vice of uncivilized peoples... to be replaced by labor systems, cultural values and religion transplanted by the conquering and superior British... until 1919 the British themselves remained addicted to a form of bondage – indentured labor – which... involved an international maritime trade in humanity not totally dissimilar to the old slave trade.

27 Takaki, *Iron*, xiii, xiv.
28 Susan-Mary Grant, "Nationalism and Ethnicity: North America," in *Encyclopedia of Race and Racism*, ed. Patrick L. Mason, 2nd ed., Vol. 3 (New York: Macmillan Reference USA, 2013), 225–229, *Gale Virtual Reference Library*, http://link.galegroup.com/apps/doc/CX4190600317/GVRL?u=csus_main&sid=GVRL&xid=25c792bd.
29 Roger Chapman, ed., "Founding Fathers," in *Culture Wars: An Encyclopedia of Issues, Viewpoints, and Voices*, Vol. 1 (New York: M.E. Sharpe, 2010), 192–193, *Gale Virtual Reference Library*, http://link.galegroup.com/apps/doc/CX1724100177/GVRL?u=csus_main&sid=GVRL&xid=7bf0cf7. Grant.
30 Lipsitz, 264.
31 Ben Knight, "Right-wing AfD Poaching Voters from German Left Part," *DW*, May 26, 2016, www.dw.com/en/right-wing-afd-poaching-voters-from-german-left-party/a-19285067. *BBC News*, "Europe and Nationalism: A Country-by-Country Guide," Sept. 10, 2018, www.bbc.com/news/world-europe-36130006. "AfD: What You Need to Know about Germany's Far-Right Party," *DW*, Sept. 24, 2017, www.dw.com/en/afd-what-you-need-to-know-about-germanys-far-right-party/a-37208199. DW, "Record-low Support for Angela Merkel's Government," Oct. 18, 2018, www.dw.com/en/record-low-support-for-angela-merkels-government/a-45950376. *BBC News*, "Germany Shocked by Cologne New Year Gang Assaults on Women," Jan. 5, 2016, www.bbc.com/news/world-europe-35231046.
32 Henry A. Giroux, "White Nationalism, Armed Culture and State Violence in the Age of Donald Trump," *Philosophy and Social Criticism* 43, no. 9 (2017): 889.
33 Giroux, 889. See Tony Badger, "New Deal," in *Encyclopedia of the Great Depression*, ed. Robert S. McElvaine, Vol. 2 (New York: Macmillan Reference USA, 2004), 701–711, *Gale Virtual Reference Library*, http://link.galegroup.com/apps/doc/CX3404500395/GVRL?u=csus_main&sid=GVRL&xid=61d8392b. The Roosevelt administration developed the New Deal as a set of programs and policies in response to the Great Depression of the 1930s.
34 United States Office of the Federal Register, "Executive Order 9102: Establishing the War Relocation Authority in the Executive Office of

the President and Defining Its Functions and Duties," March 20, 1942, Utah University Libraries Digital History Collections Topaz Japanese-American Relocation Center Digital Collection, Accessed Nov. 20, 2018, http://digital.lib.usu.edu/cdm/ref/collection/Topaz/id/69. Richard S. Nishimoto, *Inside an American Concentration Camp: Japanese American Resistance at Poston, Arizona*, ed. Lane Ryo Hirabayashi (Tucson: University of Arizona Press, 1995), xxi. In regard to the term "concentration camp" and to distinguish it from "internment camp," Hirabayashi states,

> It is . . . relevant here that the term *internment camp* (along with its derivation *internee*) is technically inappropriate for the W[ar] R[elocation] A[uthority] camps because the United States Department of Justice set up and ran special maximum-security camps to imprison Japanese, Italian and German nationals who had been swept up in the weeks following the attack on Pearl Harbor and whose loyalties were deemed suspect. These special camps were called internment camps by the Justice Department, and this convention has generally been followed in the scholarly literature to differentiate them from the camps run by the WRA.

35 Orin Starn, "Engineering Internment: Anthropologists and the War Relocation Authority," *American Ethnologist* 13, no. 4 (1986): 706.

36 Warwick Anderson, *Colonial Pathologies: American Tropical Medicine, Race, and Hygiene in the Philippines* (Durham, NC: Duke University Press, 2006), 7.

37 Joan W. Scott, "Gender: A Useful Category of Historical Analysis," *The American Historical Review* 91, no. 5 (1986): 1053–1075, quoted in Dean, 5.

38 Takaki, *Hiroshima*, 8–9. Takaki concludes that, along with President Truman's inability to comprehend Japanese people's humanity and his desire to send a message to Joseph Stalin, his insecurities about his masculinity and his attempt to compensate for them were germane to his atomic bomb mandate.

39 Ibid., 8–9. C. Wright Mills, *The Sociological Imagination* (New York: Oxford University Press, 1959).

40 Dean, 5.

41 Ibid., 10. The Stimson Center, "About Henry L. Stimson," Sept. 3, 2018, www.stimson.org/content/about-henry-l-stimson. Henry L. Stimson (1867–1950) was a lawyer and statesman who served four U.S. presidents.

42 Dean, 4, 5, 6, 169.

43 Richard Drinnon, *Keeper of Concentration Camps: Dillon S. Myer and American Racism* (Berkeley: University of California Press, 1987), 50–61.

44 Mills.

2 Overview of World War II policies targeting Japanese Americans

Chapter 2 outlines U.S. World War II policies related to Japanese Americans' human rights and civil rights violations including their forced removal from California, Washington, Oregon, and Arizona; incarceration in War Relocation Authority (WRA) camps and limited options for leaving the camps during the war. The indefinite leave policy, which the WRA also euphemistically referred to as "resettlement" and "relocation," was a top priority for the WRA's first director, Milton Eisenhower, and for Dillon S. Myer who directed the agency during most of its existence. The majority of Japanese Americans forced from the West Coast by President Roosevelt's Executive Order 9066 remained imprisoned throughout the war, but the WRA dispersed a third of the population into the Midwest and East Coast via indefinite leave. Reflecting the influence of government officials, agribusiness, and regional politicians, many people also temporarily left the camps to provide agricultural labor under the "seasonal leave" policy. Indefinite leave provides insight into national identity, whiteness, theories on race, and assimilation and on how those theories were implemented. The policy impacted people who were released from the camps, those whose indefinite leave applications were not approved, and those who, out of fear of poverty and racism, did not want to leave the camps.

Many books about Japanese Americans' wartime incarceration include the prewar years and explain what Greg Robinson refers to as the "climate of hostility," which led to the forced removal and incarceration. Robinson highlights the U.S. government's extensive surveillance of Japanese Americans years before World War II. He also emphasizes the site selection and construction of what government officials referred to as "concentration camps." They intended these camps to hold "enemy aliens," which was their term for people who were not U.S. citizens and were nationals of an enemy country. Robinson points out that the government did not have a plan, prior to the Pearl Harbor bombing, to incarcerate all Japanese Americans on the West Coast.[1] Considering the limits of space and the purpose of this monograph, I incorporate only limited aspects of the pre-World War II history, and this chapter starts with December 1941.

On December 8, 1941, the day after the Japanese military bombed Pearl Harbor, the United States declared war on Japan and placed restrictions on all Japanese Americans. By the morning of December 9, the Federal Bureau of Investigation (FBI) had arrested 1,212 Japanese men whom FBI officials considered potential threats to U.S. national security. The Justice Department incarcerated these men in detention centers and established parallel centers for Germans and Italians.[2]

On February 19, President Franklin D. Roosevelt (FDR) signed Executive Order 9066. According to this order, "the successful prosecution of the war required every possible protection against sabotage and espionage" and the Secretary of War had the authority to establish military areas "from which any or all persons may be excluded and with respect to which, the right of any person to enter, remain in or leave, shall be subjected to . . . the Secretary of War . . ."[3] Although the executive order names no specific "persons," FDR, his cabinet, and military leaders had marked Japanese Americans as the target of this executive order.

On March 2, 1942, Lieutenant General John L. DeWitt, head of the Western Defense Command, designated the western half of California, Oregon, and Washington and the southern third of Arizona as a military area and commanded that all persons of Japanese descent be removed from that area on April 30. On March 18, FDR issued Executive Order 9102 establishing the WRA as the agency empowered "to provide for the removal from designated areas of persons whose removal is necessary in the interests of national security. . ." FDR also charged the WRA with supplying the removed persons' "needs," "supervis[ing] their activities," and acquiring them "useful employment."[4] He appointed Milton S. Eisenhower from the United States Department of Agriculture as the WRA's director.

Legal scholar Jerry Kang explains that, at the end of March 1942, "the military issued a series of 100 exclusion orders, which funneled Japanese Americans, neighborhood by neighborhood, first into temporary assembly centers, then to what were euphemistically called 'relocation' camps."[5] This history is abundant with euphemisms. "Assembly centers" were ad hoc concentration camps. Many who had lived in Los Angeles, for example, found themselves forced into horse stalls at the Santa Anita racetrack cum "assembly centers" on the outskirts of town.[6]

Soon after, agribusiness leaders had hired some Japanese Americans from inside these camps. On May 21, the Army temporarily released 15 Japanese Americans from the Portland Assembly Center in Oregon for agricultural work. "Seasonal leave" to work in agriculture would become a WRA policy.

After much debate and controversy, the federal government established ten WRA camps and transported Japanese Americans to them by train. The most western camps were in California, and one was as far south and east as Arkansas. On May 8, 1942, the first WRA camp opened in Poston, Arizona.[7]

On August 7, 1942, Lieutenant General DeWitt announced that he had removed 110,000 Japanese Americans from their West Coast homes and that these individuals were either in the "assembly centers" or in the WRA concentration camps.[8] This population was entirely civilian and comprised of people of all genders. Two-thirds were American citizens under the age of 18. Those in the WRA camps did not include the 1,212 men, which the FBI had rounded up in December 1941.

The WRA camps' populations were often in flux. Transporting people from western California, Oregon, and Washington and southern Oregon to the camps was a lengthy process. Also, from the outset, people participated in "seasonal leave." In October 1942, over 8,000 Japanese Americans were temporarily released for "seasonal leave."[9]

Upon his appointment as WRA director in March 1942, Milton Eisenhower had started collaborating with civil society leaders. With them, he explored ways to release Japanese Americans from the camps for reasons other than "seasonal leave" while staying in compliance with the executive order, which made it illegal for Japanese Americans to return to their home regions. On May 29, Eisenhower established the National Student Relocation Council to move young people out of the camps and into colleges and universities.[10]

Two weeks later, on June 13, 1942, Eisenhower attended a dinner party hosted by Dillon and Jenness Myer. Dillon Myer and Eisenhower had worked together at the United States Department of Agriculture. Toward the end of the evening, Eisenhower suggested that Myer take over his position as WRA director. Two days later, Myer accepted the WRA directorship. FDR officially appointed him on June 17.[11]

According to Myer, at his first weekly WRA staff meeting, staff member Tom Holland put forth the argument that the WRA should prioritize removing people from the concentration camps. After Myer's first tour of the camps during which he visited the Tule Lake and Poston camps, he was convinced that Holland was right. In *Uprooted Americans: The Japanese Americans and the War Relocation Authority,*

Myer shares how he perceived the camps after these initial visits. He described them as, "ten abnormal cities" with "populations ranging 7,000 to 20,000 each. The majority of evacuees were between 10 and 30 years of age, with a large contingent of teenagers."[12] According to Myer, it immediately became a priority to get Japanese Americans out of the "centers" as quickly as possible.

In his autobiography, he states that policies for releasing people were a priority as of July 20, 1942, which was only a month after he was appointed.[13] That month, WRA headquarters issued its first "indefinite leave" policy document. The document specified what types of Japanese Americans would be permitted to leave.[14]

Immigrants and U.S.-born Japanese Americans who had grown up in Japan were ineligible. The policy of excluding these groups was later rescinded, but the WRA would remain less likely to approve immigrants' leave applications than those of U.S.-born Japanese Americans.

In August 1942, the WRA ordered all adults to take a so-called loyalty examination, which included listing references, preferably white people, and answering a series of questions. Question 28 of the loyalty exam required immigrants to renounce their Japanese citizenship—their only citizenship. After complaints, the WRA changed the question to ask immigrants to "abide" by U.S. laws. The entire process heightened anger and fear among Japanese Americans.[15]

Once one passed the so-called loyalty test, one was eligible for the draft, to apply for indefinite leave or both depending on age, gender, and citizenship. The intelligence agencies processed the loyalty test results, then gave the WRA the go-ahead to proceed with indefinite leave.[16] Like the loyalty test, the indefinite leave process was harrowing.

Applying for indefinite leave consisted of a written application and an interview. Under oath, Japanese Americans had to provide WRA staff with the "correct" answers to questions such as, "Will you assist in the general resettlement program by staying away from large groups of Japanese?" "Will you try to develop such habits which will cause you to be accepted readily into American social groups?" and "Will you conform to the customs and dress of your new home?"[17] If Japanese Americans had visited Japan, they had to defend themselves by explaining why to the WRA staff's satisfaction. In total, applicants had to meet fourteen conditions including having places of employment and residence secured and approved by the WRA. Neither residence nor employment could be in places of "unfavorable community sentiment," and leave clearance would not be granted for people who planned to move to "military zones" in California, Washington, Oregon, and Arizona. Myer insisted that the indefinite leave policy protected Japanese Americans by assuring whites that only loyal Japanese Americans were permitted to live and work among them.[18]

The WRA attributed traits (first generation, Japanese speaking, working class, agricultural, rural, "traditional" community norms) to immigrants whom WRA staff deemed unsuitable for indefinite leave. Whereas immigrants were liabilities whose Japaneseness could undermine the WRA project, their children were prime subjects. Some traits, like one's birth country, were undeniable but others, like "traditional community norms," reflected white liberals' perceptions more than they did Japanese Americans' realities. One was more likely to leave the WRA camps during the war if one was Christian or secular, U.S.-born, spoke English as one's dominant language, was U.S.-educated and/or had lived in a city. Seventy percent of those granted indefinite leave were between the ages of 15 and 35.[19]

If people passed this "application" and had secured employment outside of the exclusion zone, the WRA permitted them to leave the camps. Most went to the East Coast or Midwest where very few Japanese Americans, or Asians of any ethnicity, had ever lived. In 1940, 90% of Japanese Americans on the U.S. mainland had lived on the West Coast.[20]

In January 1943, WRA offices in the intermountain west, which had supervised "seasonal leave," started to encourage the agricultural workers to consider indefinite leave. Later that month, the War Department announced that it would form a Japanese American Army Unit. Also, in early 1943, the WRA established offices in Chicago, Salt Lake City, Cleveland, Minneapolis, Des Moines, New York, Denver, Kansas City, Milwaukee, and Boston where staff worked with local civil society groups to find jobs for prospective Japanese American workers. Between early 1943 and early 1944, the Japanese American Joint Board, created by the War Department, reviewed the files of all adults who were U.S. citizens and eligible for indefinite leave. This Board approved 21,000 applications, made no decisions on 500, and disapproved of 12,000.[21]

On March 20, 1943, WRA headquarters authorized lead concentration camp administrators to issue indefinite leave permits for people whom the headquarters had cleared for leave. By October 1943, 15,000 Japanese Americans had left the WRA camps. By December 1944, when the exclusion orders were rescinded, an additional 20,000 had left. The total of 35,000 amounted to one-third of those originally incarcerated. Although most settled in the Midwest and East Coast, some settled in southern cities such as Savannah and New Orleans. About 12,000 young Japanese Americans spent the duration of the war in Chicago.[22]

In April 1943, resistance to indefinite leave in the Jerome, Arkansas, camp was increasing and people were spreading stories about the problems which others were facing after taking indefinite leave. In May, a WRA staff member reported that people at Gila River, Arizona, were resisting indefinite leave and writing people in other camps advising them to not leave unless the WRA offered more support. At that point, the financial support for those leaving was $25.00 per capita, bus fare and a $3 per diem while traveling to their destinations. Having observed Japanese Americans' anger at the indefinite leave policy, some staff suggested that those who had been farmers be released to farm and be given financial support as well as that releasing people in groups instead of as individuals or in nuclear families might be more successful. A WRA social scientist, Edgar McVoy, wrote, ". . . the WRA has been much opposed to the prospect of farming more Little Tokyos such that it probably will not reverse its position with regard to group resettlement to more than a limited extent."[23] He was right.

In the effort to get more people to take indefinite leave, in early 1944, the WRA deterred people from taking "seasonal leave" by prohibiting them from returning to the WRA camp during their work contracts and capping seasonal leave permits to two per person per year. "Trial leaves" were also instituted whereby one could return to the WRA camp after four months or in the fifth or sixth months of indefinite leave. On June 12, 1944, frustrated by the slow leave rate, Myer instructed his staff to make indefinite leave their highest priority. That month, he issued a memo ordering that pro-leave material be sent to the camps and that staff disseminate the materials face-to-face as well as via pamphlets.[24]

By mid-1944, 85,000 people who had passed the loyalty test were still in WRA camps. Many of them did not want to expose themselves and their families to the risks of financial uncertainty and racism. Others had passed the loyalty test, but the WRA had not approved their indefinite leave applications.[25]

The War Department rescinded the exclusion orders on December 17, 1944. Myer still wanted Japanese Americans to voluntarily stay away from the West Coast. Continuing to believe that they needed to disperse and assimilate, he tried to deter people from returning home by warning them of the housing shortages there and emphasizing opportunities elsewhere. Despite that many Japanese Americans requested it, Myer opposed additional financial support for people who needed it so that they and their families could return to the West Coast. In March 1946, Tule Lake, the last WRA camp closed, and the WRA was terminated on June 30, 1946.[26]

By examining the intersection between the WRA and its director, Dillon Myer, Chapter 3 explores how masculinity ideologies shaped

WRA policies. How did these ideologies impact civilian policies in a time of war? What was the social, historical context which shaped the WRA's assimilationist agenda and Myer, its chief policy architect?

Notes

1 Greg Robinson, Jerry Kang, and Hiroshi Motomura, "A Symposium on Greg Robinson's A Tragedy of Democracy: Japanese Confinement in North America," *Asian Pacific American Law Journal* 15, no. 1 (June, 2010): 7.

2 J. Edgar Hoover to Edwin M. Watson, "FDR and Japanese American Internment," December 10, 1941, Franklin D. Roosevelt Presidential Library and Museum, Accessed Nov. 20, 2018, www.fdrlibrary.marist. edu/archives/pdfs/internment.pdf. "World War II Enemy Alien Control Program Overview," July 12, 2018, National Archives, Accessed Nov. 20, 2018, www.archives.gov/research/immigration/enemy-aliens-overview.

3 "Executive Order 9066," Feb. 19, 1942, National Archives, Accessed Nov. 20, 2018. www.archives.gov/historical-docs/todays-doc/?dod-date=219.

4 Ronald Takaki, *A Different Mirror: A History of Multicultural America* (New York: Back Bay Books, 2008), 344. United States Office of the Federal Register, "Executive Order 9102: Establishing the War Relocation Authority in the Executive Office of the President and Defining Its Functions and Duties," March 20, 1942, Utah University Libraries Digital History Collections Topaz Japanese-American Relocation Center Digital Collection, Accessed Nov. 20, 2018, http://digital.lib.usu.edu/cdm/ref/collection/Topaz/id/69.

5 Endo, 323 U.S. at 288, Act of Mar. 21, 1942 and Military Areas or Zones, Restrictions Pub. L. No. 77–503, 56 Stat. 173 (1942), both cited in Jerry Kang, "Watching the Watchers: Enemy Combatants in the Internment's Shadow," *Law and Contemporary Problems* 68, no. 2 (2005): 255, 280, https://scholarship.law.duke.edu/lcp/vol68/iss2/.

6 Roger Daniels, Sandra C. Taylor, and Harry H.L. Kitano, eds., *Japanese Americans: From Relocation to Redress* (Seattle: University of Washington Press, 1991), 125.

7 Takaki, *A Different Mirror*, 346. Daniels, Taylor, and Kitano, xxi.

8 Daniels, Taylor, and Kitano, xix.

9 Ibid., xix. Roger Daniels, "The Forced Migration of West Coast Japanese, 1942–1946: A Quantitative Note," in *Japanese Americans: From Evacuation to Redress*, ed. Roger Daniels, Sandra C. Taylor, and Harry H.L. Kitano (Salt Lake City: Utah of University Press, 1986), 72–74. Daniels calculates that there were 120,313 people "ever under WRA control." This number includes the 5,918 babies born in the camps.

10 *New York Times*, "Milton S. Eisenhower Dies at 85: Served as Advisor to President," May 3, 1985, www.nytimes.com/1985/05/03/us/milton-s-eisenhower-dies-at-85-served-as-adviser-to-president.html.

11 Dillon S. Myer, *An Autobiography of Dillon S. Myer* (Berkeley: University of California, 1970), 3, 6.

12 Dillon S. Myer, *Uprooted Americans: The Japanese Americans and the War Relocation Authority during World War II* (Tucson: University of Arizona Press, 1971), 32.

13 Ibid., 6. Myer, *An Autobiography*, 189.

14 United States War Relocation Authority, *The Relocation Program* (Washington, D.C.: U.S. Government Printing Office, 1946). United States War Relocation Authority, *WRA: A Story of Human Conservation* (Washington, D.C.: U.S. Government Printing Office, 1946). The WRA used "resettlement" and "relocation" interchangeably to describe the forced removal from the West Coast and departure from WRA camps after the Army lifted the exclusion orders in 1945. Government officials used "indefinite leave," "resettlement" and "relocation" interchangeably to describe release from a WRA camp during the war and leaving once the exclusion orders were lifted.

15 Greg Robinson, *By Order of the President: FDR and the Internment of Japanese Americans* (Cambridge, MA: Harvard University Press, 2001), 180–181.

16 Dorothy Swaine Thomas with Charles Kikuchi and James Minoru Sakoda, *The Salvage* (Berkeley, CA: University of California Press, 1952), 108.

17 Myer, *Uprooted Americans*, xiv. Michi Weglyn, *Years of Infamy: The Untold story of America's Concentration Camps* (New York: William Morrow and Co., 1976).

18 Myer, *Uprooted Americans*, xiv.

19 Thomas, Kikuchi, and Sakoda, 115–128.

20 Roger Daniels, *Concentration Camps, USA: Japanese Americans and World War II* (New York: Holt, Rinehart and Winston, 1971), 166–167.

21 Hearings Before A Subcommittee on Military Affairs of the United States Senate—78th Congress, First Session on Jan. 20, 27, and 28 1943 S. 444 p.83, WRA Memoranda and Reports 1943–1946, Myer Papers, Truman Library, Independence, MO. Thomas, Kikuchi, and Sakoda, 109–110. The Joint Board was comprised of a representative each from the WRA, Office of Naval Intelligence and the Provost Marshal General's office.

22 United States War Relocation Authority, *The Relocation Program*, 45, 86. Thomas, Kikuchi, and Sakoda, 105, 106.

23 Ibid., 109. Edgar McVoy to John Embree, May 6, 1943, Records of the United States War Relocation Authority, MS 42, Special Collections, University of Arizona Library, Tucson. Edgar McVoy to John Embree, Aug. 2, 1943, Edgar McVoy, Records of the United States War Relocation Authority, MS 42, Special Collections, University of Arizona Library, Tucson. Leland Barrow, Acting Director, WRA to all project directors, Oct. 28, 1943, WRA Papers Headquarters-Subject-Classified Gen. Files, File 2 Jan. to Dec. 1943, 71.100, RG 210, National Archives Building, Washington, D.C.

24 Thomas, Kikuchi, and Sakoda, 111–112. WRA Headquarters, June 6, 1943, WRA Paper Headquarters-Subject-Classified General, Jan. to Dec. 1943, 71.100, RG 210, National Archives Building, Washington, D.C.

25 Thomas, Kikuchi, and Sakoda, 105–127.

26 Jerry Kang, "Denying Prejudice: Internment, Redress, and Denial," *UCLA Law Review* 51, no. 933 (2004): 959, 960. Myer, *Uprooted Americans*, xxix. Daniels, Taylor, and Kitano, xxi.

Photo 1 Corporal Shohara on a Visit to His Parents, WRA Manzanar Camp, 1943.

Source: Adams, Ansel, photographer. *Corporal Jimmie Shohara, Manzanar Relocation Center / photograph by Ansel Adams.* California Manzanar, 1943. Photograph. https://www.loc.gov/item/2001704602/.

Photo 2 Corporal Shohara's Ribbons, 1943.

Source: Adams, Ansel, photographer. *Corporal Jimmie Shohara's ribbons, Manzanar Relocation Center / photograph by Ansel Adams.* California Manzanar, 1943. Photograph. https://www.loc.gov/item/2002695980/.

Photo 3 Yonemitsu Family Pictures and Mementoes, WRA Manzanar Camp, 1943.

Source: Adams, Ansel, photographer. *Pictures and mementoes on phonograph top: Yonemitsu home, Manzanar Relocation Center / photograph by Ansel Adams.* California Manzanar, 1943. Photograph. https://www.loc.gov/item/2002695978/.

3 Dillon Myer goes to war
Masculinity and the War Relocation Authority

In a letter to a Japanese American soldier, War Relocation Authority (WRA) director, Dillon Myer, portrays himself and his WRA endeavors with martial metaphors and masculinist rhetoric:

> The WRA and the forces of good will have been definitely on the offensive for the past several months and the . . . boys . . . have supplied us with guns and ammunition to carry on the fight . . . Naturally, many bigots are still in existence and the war has not been completely won, but we are winning the major battles now . . .

Writing in December 1944, Myer's "war" was in its third year. The "boys" were Japanese American soldiers who had enlisted in the U.S. Army from inside WRA concentration camps. Their combat duty, replete with record casualties and mortalities, served the WRA and its allies as "guns and ammunition" in a war over American culture and identity.[1]

Many of Myer's white-collar performances of masculinity rested on other men's bodies suffering the assaults of war. He represented himself as a warrior who heroically fought to rescue Japanese Americans. One of Myer's earliest victories was the reclassification of young Japanese American men from "enemy aliens" so that they would be eligible for the draft. Whether by elite or general cultural standards, Myer became more masculine as World War II progressed and he "won battles."[2] In his own estimation, "when I took over the Directorship of the War Relocation Authority . . . I lost all feeling of insecurity. . ."[3]

Winning battles in this culture war entailed engaging in a politics of recognition shaped by gender and nationalist ideologies. The America for which Myer and the "forces of goodwill" were fighting was in direct opposition to that of his "enemies."[4] Contemporary policy options included Tennessee Senator Stewart's bill to incarcerate all persons of Japanese ancestry for World War II's duration and Oregon Senator Holman's bill to strip U.S.-born Japanese Americans of their citizenship.[5]

Myer and his allies aimed to convince white Americans that Japanese Americans were assimilated to white middle-class culture. Then, according to his strategy, whites would cease to view Japanese Americans as threats to national security and consent to them living, at liberty, among other Americans. In recognizing Japanese Americans, liberals sought to disrupt, but not abandon, the dominant national identity.

WRA policy responded to this national identity by rejecting its whites-only, but not its patriarchal, element. Myer promoted a narrative, which placed Japanese Americans into the national story casting them as familiar, approachable, and prosaic. Operating within a male-centered national identity, he sought to transform Japanese Americans' image by depicting them as "the boy next door" or as "G.I. Joe," the boy next door serving his country.

These iconic personifications of national identity directly contradict the yellow peril stereotype according to which Asians are inherently threatening and unassimilable. Paradoxically, this stereotype depicts Asian men as effeminate and attributes to them high levels of traits which American elites associated with masculinity. These traits include stoicism, intelligence, and military strategic abilities so great that Asians are supposedly, as Charles Vevier phrases it, "always on the point of invading and destroying Christendom, Europe, and Western civilization itself."[6]

Japanese American soldiers served as the linchpin of the indefinite leave policy though which the WRA would eventually allow 35,000 Japanese Americans to leave its camps during the war. Their participation in U.S. military warfare was a violence of inclusion into the U.S. body politic. Arguing against Japanese Americans' literal and metaphoric exclusion, Myer used soldiers' combat records in confronting his enemies—"bigots," conservative congressmen, and the anti-Japanese American media—who threatened the WRA agenda and his personal inclusion in elite politics.[7]

As WRA director, Myer enjoyed his first Presidential appointment and entered the exclusive Bourgeois Brotherhood, which included Harry Truman and select other white men who had been born into middle-class families. He gained access to this Brotherhood through an old boys' network, which he and other college-educated white men operationalized as a de facto affirmative action program for each other and themselves. In order to understand Myer's role in the culture war, it is necessary to understand the middle-class, patriarchal culture which dominated the U.S. before and during World War II.

From an old boys' network

Bourgeois Brothers mobilized regional old boys' networks to build their careers and connect to the political elite. Profiting from whiteness, they cashed in on systems composed of, as Lipsitz explains, "insider networks that channel employment opportunities to the relatives and friends of those who have profited most from present and past racial discrimination."[8] As a student at the Ohio State University, Myer joined a middling status fraternity that made him part of a Midwestern network, which would provide him a series of opportunities and, eventually, entrée into the Bourgeois Brotherhood.[9] This network and Myer's entrance into the Brotherhood demonstrate the white, patriarchal culture which shaped the WRA.

While much less exclusive than those of the Imperial Brotherhood, members of old boys' networks also shared institutions that instilled masculinity ideologies. These institutions paralleled those of the Imperials and included universities, fraternities, offices, and private clubs, which Myer's old boys had in common along with naming practices, Protestantism, and migration to urban America. These institutions and traits were part of their fraternal imagined community, an informal, middle-class association of white men strengthened in written correspondence, private homes, and government agencies.[10] Extending across the nation and into U.S. colonies, this network, like the Imperial and Bourgeois Brotherhoods, reflected and shaped white professional men's dominant relationships to other groups including women, Native Americans, African Americans, Filipinos, and Japanese Americans.

Most men in Myer's network came from families who benefitted from the United States' westward expansion, the ideology of manifest destiny, and a national economy developed by enslaving Africans and seizing Natives' land. In 1891, Myer was born in rural Ohio to parents who were community leaders and had inherited a 135-acre farm. The farm was an example of that especially lucrative form of the "possessive investment in whiteness," "intergenerational transfers of inherited wealth that pass[ed] on the spoils of discrimination to succeeding generations."[11] These families also bequeathed patriarchal norms to their children. They were more likely to send their sons than their daughters to college. Seeped in hierarchies, Myer's childhood would correlate in many ways with his WRA directorship.[12]

Men in old boys' networks spent much of their professional and social lives in exclusively male and male-dominated institutions. As boys, they attended public schools with girls, but their lives became increasingly male-centered when they entered university. Myer was among the first generation of middle-class men who went to college in large numbers. Attending land grant universities, these young men left behind rural cultures, which, while patriarchal, accorded women substantial roles as providers. The young men entered an increasingly male-centered world, which would herald that of their futures.[13]

After graduating from high school, Myer moved to Columbus to attend the Ohio State University where he gained access to increasingly higher social status despite a lackluster academic record. He writes in his autobiography that, on his first day as an undergraduate, he met an Alpha Zeta fraternity brother and accepted a lunch invitation to the fraternity house. Myer went on to pledge Alpha Zeta and credited it with helping him academically and professionally: "I had some wonderful friends among this group plus a great deal of contact with agricultural leaders who had graduated from the fraternity and in many ways I profited from having been a member of the organization."[14] Living in the fraternity house, Myer spent many evenings playing cards and going to the movies.[15] Whether or not he was aware of it at the time, his heavy socializing cultivated a network of college-educated men, which would benefit his career.

As a sophomore, Myer decided to major in agronomy after a professor and Alpha Zeta alumnus told him that, if he did, the professor would make sure Myer had a job when he graduated. When he was a senior, another fraternity brother recommended Myer for a teaching job at the University of Kentucky which the brother was leaving for one at Kansas State College. Despite that Myer had just flunked an agronomy final, Arthur McCall, Ohio State's head of agronomy, recommended him for the Kentucky position. In 1914, the year that World War I began, Myer finished his baccalaureate and started his career. Beginning with that Kentucky job, his old boys' network consistently recommended and recruited Myer for positions and promotions.[16]

Years later, in 1947, McCall became the National Director of Agricultural Extension in Washington, D.C. and co-sponsored Myer into the Cosmos Club. His Cosmos Club membership symbolizes Myer's social climb. Elite professional status and being a man were requirements for membership. Male scientists, intellectuals, and high-ranking public servants established the Club in the 1870s. Still in existence in 2018, the Club began to admit women in 1988—six years after Myer's death.[17] The Cosmos Club demonstrates that, while members of Myer's network had much less privilege than wealthy men, they had much more than most people. Neither the Club nor middle-class old boys' networks welcomed poor or working-class people, women, or people of color.

In 1916, Myer moved from the University of Kentucky back to Ohio to work as an agriculture extension agent. The following year, while many other young men were at war, members of Myer's network, Purdue University professors, secured him a civilian position as an emergency wartime Assistant County Agent Leader. Myer accepted the position and skipped military service, which was a significant aspect of his generations' white American masculinity.[18]

Myer was aware of the status of military and, especially, combat duty. During World Wars I and II, segregation largely limited combat's prestige to white men. According to the hegemonic order, women and African Americans, the "central" minority group in U.S. history, were incapable of combat and gay men were barred from the military altogether.[19] With these exclusions, warfare legitimated heterosexual white men's dominant role in the United States. Overwhelmingly, they were the ones whom the nation celebrated for sacrificing life and limb.[20]

Although he missed the military rite of passage, Myer did not miss marriage or fatherhood, which were other important rites of passage. In 1924, he proposed to his future wife, Jenness Wirt, who had already planned to finish her fine arts degree at Columbia University. The couple moved in 1925, and Myer also enrolled in Columbia where he earned a Master of Arts in Education. On Myer's salaries, they would go on to raise three daughters in suburban Washington, D.C. Myer's family life and career symbolized his culture's conception of, what Suzik terms, "manly independence and strength."[21]

While the physical and emotional trauma of World War I contributed to many Americans' rejection of war as a fundamental part of manhood, the Great Depression's mass unemployment underscored providing for one's family as crucial to men's roles. Many men suffered from crises having lost their jobs, farms, and roles as providers. In 1933, the Roosevelt administration created the Civilian Conservation Core to provide work, not military, training to catalyze boys into manhood. In this context, Myer's lack of military service did not threaten his masculinity, and his consistent employment and promotions bolstered it.[22]

A husband and father in the 1930s, Myer supported his family by working in New Deal agriculture programs. As a white-collar professional with two university degrees, he was fully employed throughout

the Depression, and his career flourished amid unprecedented government agricultural programs. In Ohio, he worked in the Agricultural
Adjustment Administration (AAA).[23]

In 1934, Myer moved to Washington, D.C. to work at the AAA in the
United States Department of Agriculture (USDA) headquarters. His
next positions were as the USDA Assistant Chief in Charge of Cooperative Relations and Information for the Soil Conservation Service and,
then, as Chief of the Division of Cooperative Relations and Planning.
These roles involved public relations and the press, allowing Myer to
build skills that he would use as WRA director. With these promotions, Myer's old boys' network grew and, among his colleagues, were
men who would later work for the WRA.[24] Together, they would apply
New Deal male-centered practices and ideas to that wartime agency.

In Washington, D.C., Myer's network included Milton Eisenhower
(1899–1985) who also worked at the USDA and who would pave Myer's
way to the WRA directorship. Eisenhower successfully advocated
for Myer's generous salary during Myer's early years in Washington,
D.C.[25] The two men shared a similar background.

Milton Eisenhower and his brothers, including future President
Dwight Eisenhower (1890–1969), grew up in rural America. Milton
graduated from Kansas State University, and like Myer, was offered
a University of Kentucky teaching position. Eisenhower, however,
joined the foreign service propelling him into more exclusive circles.
In 1926, the Kansas old boys' network brought him home from Europe
to Washington, D.C. Only two years out of college, he served as the
assistant to the USDA Secretary. Eisenhower stayed at the USDA
throughout the New Deal and until March 1942 when FDR appointed
him WRA director.[26]

Born in an agricultural area where women often held the purse
strings, Myer and others in his network transitioned from farm boys
to white collar, urban professionals and experienced the related gender role changes. Whereas on the farm, the dichotomy between public
and private was not distinct with everyone contributing to the farm/
household, industrialization, urbanization, racism, and imperialism
had produced a public–private dichotomy and related gender ideologies according to which women occupied the private space of the
home and men occupied public spaces including those of paid work.
Conforming to these roles, Myer commuted to Washington D.C. from
the suburbs while his wife managed their single-family home and children's care.[27] The head of a white, nuclear, middle-class family based
on a heterosexual couple, Myer personified many patriarchal cultural
ideals and conformed to the norms of his old boys' network.

Complementing his domestic life, Myer's professional life reflected gender roles which privileged men in more powerful and higher paying positions than women. Myer and most of his WRA staff were former USDA employees and part of the old boys' network, which had carried over from his college fraternity and the New Deal into World War II. Like most predominately male workspaces, government was male-centered, masculinized, and heteronormative. According to Connell, the state is a "masculine institution" where "[t]he overwhelming majority of top office-holders are men." The patriarchal order created "a gender configuring in recruitment and promotion, . . . in the internal division of labor and systems of control . . ."[28] The old boys' network ensured this gender configuring and that it continued into the WRA.

Myer's correspondence reveals how masculinity ideology manifested in the USDA's "internal division of labor" and "practical routines."[29] In 1938, a former colleague wrote Myer in Washington, D.C., ". . . I often wonder if you Ohio ex-extension fellows ever had occasion to meet." His reference to "fellows" speaks to the fact that their former colleagues were overwhelmingly male. The Ohioan continues by mentioning colleagues' names all of which are male and Euro-American. He then adds,

> . . . there is one more ex-extension worker in Washington, one of the girls who worked for me . . . She's a really grand secretary, too, and if you need a good one sometime you might give the Ohio girl a chance . . . Give my regards to Mrs. Myers [sic].[30]

This letter demonstrates how, as clerks and secretaries, women played support roles to men who predominated in mid- and high-level positions. Office routines included men dictating letters to women who typed men's words. A common heteronormative practice was for men to send greetings to each other's wives. The WRA would also be established as a "masculine institution" where patriarchy organized the division of labor. White men who predominated in mid- and high-level positions would formulate and implement policies, and war would become a form of labor for young Japanese American men.[31]

By the late 1930s, Europe was at war again and, in the United States, military service reemerged as primary to mainstream masculinity ideology. In 1940, Congress mandated that the Civilian Conservation Core provide men and boys noncombat military training. After the entry of United States into World War II in December 1941, G.I. Joe became a symbol of ideal masculinity.[32] Young men enlisted and, also in uniform, many men Myer's age served as officers. While Myer's domestic and professional roles were consistent with his masculinity ideology, with the United States at war again, his lack of military experience contrasted with it. His old boys' network, though, would soon provide him with a civilian opportunity with which he would uphold war's role in hegemonic masculinity.

Into the Bourgeois Brotherhood

In the Washington, D.C. suburbs, Mr. and Mrs. Myer practiced "mobilizing pleasure" or, what Rotundo calls, ". . . a form of business entertainment . . . the carefully arranged dinner party. . ."[33] Simultaneously informal and ritualized, dinner parties were common practices which overlapped with "gender configuring in recruitment and promotion." "Deliberately heterosexual," this male-centered custom included having wives in support roles similar to secretaries' roles at work. Doing gender meant wives preparing dinners, often by supervising domestic workers, then serving as hostesses to their husbands' associates and their wives.[34] These parties were typical of the old boys' network culture, which combined business and pleasure. Old boys employed the symbolic and real boundaries of private homes and clubs to control which outsiders they permitted in and to confidentially share information. It was at a dinner party that Myer learned of his opportunity to direct the WRA.

Myer and Milton Eisenhower got to know each other over the years that they both worked at the USDA. Eisenhower had stayed at the USDA until March 1942 when FDR appointed him WRA director. In June 1942, at the end of a dinner party at the Myer's home, Eisenhower lingered on chatting with the Myers. Turning the conversation to work, he explained that he had been offered the position of Deputy of the Office of War Information. Then, in this intimate setting, Eisenhower deviated from the men's shared masculinity ideology, which discouraged them from revealing vulnerabilities. He confided that he was glad to move on from the WRA as directing it had left him unable to sleep at night.[35]

After this confession, Eisenhower asked Myer if he might be interested in taking over the WRA. Within days, Myer had started his new position, which, as a Presidential appointment, marked his entrée into the Bourgeois Brotherhood. Myer wrote a friend that he was confident that the WRA directorship would not keep him from sleeping well.[36]

In addition to the status of a Presidential appointment, the WRA provided Myer a lauded wartime role. Fifty years old in 1942, for the second time, he witnessed men going off to war and, as a Presidential appointee, his professional circles included men his age who were high-ranking, active duty, military officers and World War I veterans. Myer's lack of military experience contrasted strongly with historical normative masculinity, the World War II resurgence of war's centrality to masculinity, and the elite American masculinity ideology to which war had been consistently central.[37] Fortunately for him, his old boys' network had yielded the unique position of directing the WRA directorship.

Myer's WRA policies would reflect the patriarchal state and network which led to his appointment. As students, the men socialized in fraternities which they used to establish and develop their careers. As professionals, they perpetuated patriarchal inequities through dinner parties, correspondence, and other white-collar customs.

A violence of inclusion

In his efforts to manage the public's perception of Japanese Americans, Myer contended with Congressional attacks, anti-Japanese American newspapers, and the Roosevelt administration's damage to Japanese American optics. He viewed the Hearst and other media outlets as his main enemies as they spread yellow peril propaganda and flamed white resistance to the WRA. For example, in 1942, *Time* magazine described a Japanese soldier as having raped Chinese girls and "wondering what white ones would be like."[38]

FDR and other Democrats were complicit in assisting these newspapers. By removing Japanese Americans from the West Coast and forcing them into concentration camps, the Roosevelt administration had reinforced the myth of Japanese Americans as threats. Robinson writes that FDR's "long refusal to issue a statement praising Japanese-American loyalty bore bitter fruit. Anti-Japanese-American newspapers . . . filled the vacuum. . . with invented stories of internee treachery and luxurious conditions in the camps."[39]

In addition to tackling the media, part of Myer's job was to engage in Congressional politics or, what Dean terms, "high" level "struggles over political inclusion and exclusion."[40] Congressional hearings were often contentious forums ruled by men performing masculinity in efforts to increase and maintain their political power. As a New Dealer, Myer knew what to expect of Congressional politics and approached the hearings with vigor and toughness—valued characteristics of the Imperial and Bourgeois Brotherhoods. In his exchanges with political and military leaders, Myer's performance resembled the Brotherhoods' Stimsonian ideal, which emphasized stoicism, heroism, toughness, optimism, resoluteness, and a "manly spirit" of restraint.[41]

Stoicism and optimism were characteristic of Myer's leadership style, which his staff observed and, sometimes, found frustrating. One WRA staff member wrote to her supervisor that a colleague "is still in his pessimistic binge [about the low numbers of Japanese Americans accepting indefinite leave]—in fact he went to see Mr. Myer about it . . . However, he reports that Myer didn't feel the need for suggestions and said, 'I'm more optimistic than I ever have been before.' You can see everyone is keeping in character . . ."[42] While frustrating for staff, stoicism and optimism were advantageous in the face of media attacks and the Congressional onslaught, which came from Republicans and Democrats.

Working for the USDA, Myer had had a front row seat to conservatives' attacks on Roosevelt advisor and Bourgeois Brother, Rexford G. Tugwell (1891–1979), who had initiated many New Deal agriculture programs. New Deal opponents succeeded in making Tugwell FDR's liability such that Tugwell went from being a member of the brain trust with regular access to the President to spending World War II as the governor of Puerto Rico—on the geographical and metaphorical margins of U.S. power. Once Republicans prevailed against Tugwell and he had lost in the arena of Congressional politics, he never worked in Washington D.C. again.[43]

Politicians opposed to the New Deal or to Japanese Americans, including some Democrats, threatened the WRA's policies and Myer's Presidential appointment. Some senators publicly worried that Japanese Americans endangered whites who lived near WRA camps and that the WRA might release dangerous people through a loophole. In early 1942, before FDR ordered Japanese Americans' removal, Senator Harley Kilgore, a West Virginia Democrat on the Senate Committee on Military Affairs, wrote FDR urging that the Pacific Coast be cleansed of Japanese Americans. In January 1943, West Coast senators Mon Wallgren and Rufus C. Holman introduced a bill to transfer the WRA's functions to the War Department. California Congressman William Johnson introduced a resolution to have the WRA investigated. Also, the Senate Military Affairs Subcommittee, chaired by Kentuckian Albert Chandler, investigated the WRA in a series of hearings. Chandler fanned yellow peril propaganda with impromptu press conferences and, Myer employed written propaganda to dispel the yellow peril myth.[44]

Describing his Congressional testimonies in a 1943 letter, Myer uses martial metaphors. He depicts Senate hearings as a hand-to-hand and armed combat:

> We took it on the chin . . . from the Senate Military Affairs Committee . . . and . . . the Dies Sub-Committee on Un-American

Activities . . . We had our guns loaded and took advantage of our opportunity to go on the offensive and win the battle.[45]

Countering the rumor that the WRA was "soft" on Japanese Americans, Myer argued that the military draft Japanese American men incarcerated in the camps.[46]

Unwilling to let the WRA transfer to the military, which would have cost him his Presidential appointment, Myer strengthened his position by creating a closer association with the military while keeping the WRA a civilian agency. He invoked "military masculinity," which, as Aaron Belkin explains in *Bring Me Men: Military Masculinity and the Benign Façade of American Empire, 1898–2001*, "enable[s] individuals to legitimize their authority by associating themselves with the military. . ." "Promoting martial values," "claim[ing] authority on the basis of affirmative relationships with the military" and "connect[ing] to the military" bolstered Myer's standing as trustworthy, competent and masculine.[47]

During the Senate hearings, Myer presented a military draft along with education, food, work, and the indefinite leave policy as components of the WRA's assimilation project. He insisted that once soldiers had risked their lives to gain acceptance, whites needed to "absorb" Japanese Americans. He stated that the soldiers' sacrifices would result in Americanizing Japanese Americans. Their parents would be "indoctrinated" and encouraged to adopt white cultural norms like Christianity, "American" food, and English.[48] Perceiving the parents as embodiments of Japanese heritage, Myer advocated for keeping them incarcerated while dispersing their young adult children into the Midwest and East Coast. Separated from their parents, Myer anticipated that the young adults would completely assimilate to white American culture because, "They won't know anything else."[49] From his perspective, not reinstating the draft and keeping Japanese Americans in camps "along the lines of an Indian reservation" would exacerbate the situation.[50]

On the last day of the hearings, January 28, 1943, the War Department announced that it would form a Japanese American Army unit. The 442nd Infantry Regimental Combat Team was a segregated outfit, which, starting in March 1943, included Japanese American soldiers from Hawaii as well as those directly out of WRA camps. Sent on especially dangerous missions, the 442nd became the most decorated unit in U.S. Army history although the Army did not award many of the medals until the 1990s.[51] In Myer's politics of recognition, Japanese American soldiers' sacrifices served as painful yet necessary weapons for well-intended white Americans who took the offensive on their behalf.

Belkin describes how, "the body of the soldier has come to signify the nation and national security in particularly intensified ways." Myer tapped into the World War II zeitgeist. As literary critic Christina Jarvis explains, during World War II, "the American military, government, and other institutions shaped the male body both figuratively and literally in an effort to communicate impressions of national strength to U.S. citizens and to other nations."[52] Japanese American soldiers' bodies became means of communication—texts on which to inscribe Americanness as supreme and inclusive.

Some Japanese Americans, though, would ultimately be excluded as they sacrificed their lives defending the United States.[53] Death brought literal exclusion as it increased metaphoric inclusion. Positing a male-centered Japanese American identity in response to a male-centered white American national identity, the WRA publicized Japanese American men's exceptionally high rates of combat deaths and wounds as manly sacrifices and grounds on which the white public should include Japanese Americans in U.S. national identity. Photographs of award ceremonies with grieving parents were part of Myer's strategies for winning over white Americans.

In December 1944, Myer wrote to a Japanese American soldier:

> Naturally the casualty lists wring my heart . . . I want you to know and I want everybody in the 442nd to know—that the effect of the job that is being done is tremendous . . . we have a tangible and dramatic answer to the [anti-Japanese American newspapers] . . . when they try to carry on their program based on their key cliché—namely 'A Jap is a Jap' . . .[54]

In this letter, Myer demonstrates how casualty and mortality rates were essential to his "tangible and dramatic answer" to racist newspaper publishers and other "evil forces." Thomas, Kikuchi, and Sakoda write: ". . .the unabated favorable publicity [Japanese American soldiers] received, and the contacts they established in American communities prior to overseas service were undoubtedly primary factors in promoting community acceptance of resettlers in the Middle West and East from the WRA camps."[55] In another letter written to a Japanese American soldier, Myer explains how pleased he was with the soldiers:

> . . . the 100th Battalion and the 442nd Regimental Combat Team have lived up to my fondest expectations. I only wish that you . . . and the other fellows, could see the tremendous change that has gradually taken place . . . as a result of . . . the reinstitution of

selective service. . . There have been news reels, and movie shorts, speeches. . . which have meant a great deal to the future of the Japanese American citizens in this country and to the WRA program. You fellows who are willing to risk it all certainly have a double right to be proud of the service you are rendering, not only to the country, but to the evacuee group. . . There are nearly 31,000 people on indefinite leave . . . over 5,000 others are on seasonal leave. . . The attitude on the [West] Coast and throughout the country is materially better . . .[56]

Myer depicts the soldiers as spokesmen for the larger Japanese American population and for the WRA. He correlates their military and diplomatic endeavors to Japanese Americans' releases from WRA camps and to changes in white Americans' "attitudes." With a particularly cruel twist on filial piety, Myer stresses to the soldier that families' and communities' freedom depends on him and other young men.

This politics of recognition excluded women, queer men, and immigrants as they did not fit normative masculinity or the image which Myer was trying to create. As Thangaraj says of South Asian American men in the twenty-first century, for Japanese American soldiers, "Reconfiguring racialized masculinities and performing cultural citizenship . . . require[d] the implementing of exclusion."[57] For U.S.-born Japanese American men, the WRA "fashion[ed] cultural citizenship at the intersections of masculinity, race, middle class respectability, and heterosexuality."[58]

The exchange of letters between Myer and O.G. Anderson of Tobacco By-Products and Chemical Corporation demonstrates some of the attitudes among the public. Amid friendly banter, Anderson suggests that Myer gas Japanese Americans:

I thought it was too bad to have such a good man . . . wasting his time on the yellow race . . . you may need some means of self-defense against the jujitsu when Japs are around. We could recommend our Nico-Fume Pressure Fumigators. Once lighted [sic], they would most certainly keep the Yellow Peril at a safe distance. But I don't suppose the New Deal would let you use it, because it might be construed as a sort of "gas attack."[59]

Gendered speech marks the letter's alternatively warm and combative tones. Anderson refers to Myer as a "good man" and closes with the masculine white-collar ritual greeting to Mrs. Myer. He makes overtly racist statements, expresses his hostility toward Japanese Americans, and takes a jab at the New Deal. The suggestion to use Nico-Fume

Pressure Fumigators is disturbing considering that, at the time of this correspondence, Nazis were murdering Jews with gas.

Remaining courteous, Myer addresses the genocidal suggestion by pointing out its problems:

> It happens that the descendants of the yellow race with whom I am dealing are mostly citizens . . . to many people throughout the country a "Jap is a Jap" . . . [I think some people forget] just what is in the Constitution and the Bill of Rights . . . I certainly did appreciate your letter and hope this war will be over some time . . . so we can begin to see old friends again.[60]

Before his diplomatic closing, Myer describes how he enjoys his WRA work implying that his talents were being put to good use. He positions the WRA and Japanese Americans as part of American national identity and related to the Constitution and the Bill of Rights, some of the most potent U.S. symbols, while implying that Anderson and conservatives are un-American. Couched in congenial small talk, which maintains their old boys' network ties, Myer's response to Anderson addresses Anderson's political jab and racist ideas without insulting him. Did Myer really appreciate Anderson's letter? Did he consider him an "old friend" and look forward to seeing him again? Regardless of the answers to those questions, Myer responded to Anderson's gendered speech with strategically restrained aggression in accordance with the Brotherhoods' masculinity ideology.

Masculine narratives

Myer's contemporary and Bourgeois Brother, President Truman, consistently presented himself as tough to manage feelings of inferiority, which stemmed from his youth when his family and other boys treated him as feeble and feminine. By World War II, he had fulfilled many of his masculinity ideologies' criteria including Word War I combat duty as a commanding officer. Nonetheless, the insecurities which had plagued him since boyhood manifested in displays of bravado during international war negotiations, and they increased his motivation to drop atomic bombs. Truman's practice of "masculine diplomacy" lends credence to Boyle's assertion that ". . . warrior identities can be so closely aligned with ideas about masculinity that some American presidents have been motivated to wage war to demonstrate their masculinity."[61] Myer shared Truman's masculinity ideology and, by his own admission, Myer had suffered from feelings of insecurity until he won "battles" during World War II. In his autobiography, he states that he "lost all feelings of insecurity" when he took over the WRA.[62]

President Truman associated regret with vulnerability and femininity and, therefore, hid regret about the U.S. atomic bombings of Hiroshima and Nagasaki behind a public mask of resolve. Similarly, Myer claimed to have no regrets about his actions during World War II, and he offered no critique of himself or of the WRA. In the media, correspondence, Congressional testimonies, his autobiography and his book, *Uprooted Americans: The Japanese Americans and the War Relocation Authority During World War II*, it is difficult to detect compassion for the people who suffered under his administration.[63]

As Secretary of War Henry Stimson said of the decision to drop atomic bombs: "'No single individual can hope to know exactly what took place in the minds of all of those who shared these events . . .'"[64] It is, also, impossible to know exactly what took place in Myer's mind. Clearly, though, he operated in a world which linked emotional control with masculinity, and he left behind written records with a paucity of emotions.[65] Whether that of his old boys' network or the Brotherhoods, the masculinity ideologies prevalent in Myer's social worlds motivated men to avoid displays of emotions. For men like Myer and Truman whose careers depended on conforming to masculinity ideals, there was little space to critique one's self privately much less publicly. Professionally, men in their milieu benefitted from concealing vulnerabilities and minimizing their risk of losing status.

As Truman did in international negotiations, with his communication style, Myer performed masculinity. A man whom powerful men associated with liberal, and even pro-Japanese stances during World War II, Myer experienced "great pressures toward conformity to dominant ideologies of masculinity" and used conforming behavior in countering attacks.[66] During World War II and in the books which he wrote almost 30 years later, Myer evokes military masculinity and overwhelmingly portrays himself as a warrior who triumphed over foes as varied as agricultural pests and yellow peril propaganda.[67]

In contrast to Milton Eisenhower, Myer prided himself on his ability to sleep soundly as WRA director. About Eisenhower, he states,

> . . . he did not like to get in between a rock and a hard place. . . in this [WRA] job. . . the pressures on both sides were very, very heavy and this upset him very much.

Regarding himself, Myer claims, "the pressure from racists and from the people who were trying to beat us to the ground all of the time" was of little significance to him. He states, "I was able to take [the pressure] all in stride and fortunately I have always been a good sleeper . . ."[68]

In reflecting on his time as an agricultural instructor at the University of Kentucky, Myer reveals that his mentors' trust was critical to developing his self-confidence. Already suffering from insecurity in his professional roles, Myer reveals that, during World War I, he felt ashamed at being a civilian. In his autobiography, he divulges,

> I found myself in quite an embarrassing situation, because I was not in uniform . . . every time I saw a troop train full of men in uniform . . . and I was in civies [sic] I felt that I was a slacker. Much to my surprise however, I was never accosted with such a charge during World War I or since.[69]

Myer expected young men in uniform to harass him and worried that others would see him as a man who was evading his duty. Fifty years after World War I, he expresses surprise that he had never been harassed as a draft dodger.

Myer writes that he first turned down the emergency agricultural position, which kept him out of World War I: ". . . I felt that I should join the Army. . ."[70] He states that he would have preferred to enlist.

> . . . I learned that [the professors] without saying anything to me had proceeded to get me reclassified. . . I was told that my experience and ability was more important to the government . . . than service to the Army. So I reluctantly accepted . . . on three or four different occasions . . . I [planned] . . . to go into the Army. Each time [my boss] urged that I stay . . .[71]

According to Myer, the deferred classification was completed without his knowledge, and he felt uncomfortable about it. He traveled to Purdue University several times specifically to resign but, each time, he complied with his bosses' wishes instead. He depicts himself as a dutiful young man who submitted to the requests of his professional father figures despite his own inclinations. Had Myer served in the military, he would have fulfilled a significant requirement of his masculinity ideology and, perhaps, gone a long way toward resolving his insecurities.

Perhaps in lieu of military service, Myer depicts his World War I agricultural work as replete with sacrifices:

> . . . during most of the war period I traveled from the first of the week to the weekend. . . I get tired even yet when I think about

how tired I was at times. Those long hours, lack of sleep with the grinding work . . . w[ere] required and something that we didn't think too much about at that time.[72]

In an autobiography, which chronicles every job he held, the World War I job is the only one which Myer describes as tiring much less "exhausting." His description of his fatigue is a "structuring contradiction," which supports his masculinity ideology.[73] Admitting that he suffered from fatigue may seem to contradict his masculinity ideology, but the narrative reads that he was heroic. He was tough enough to sacrifice for the war effort. As he had sacrificed, he could not have been a weakling or a "slacker."

With his World War I story, Myer explains why he deviated from the ideal narrative of serving his country. According to Dean, "erasing, repressing, or explaining away deviations from ideal master narratives" is common in ambitious men's stories about themselves.[74] Belkin explains that the ideology of military masculinity produces "conformity and obedience." "Embodying masculinity" required Myer to "enter into intimate relationships with. . . unmasculine foils, not just to disavow them." In Myer's "pursuit of masculine status," he disavowed "the unmasculine," not serving in the military, "via the compelled embrace of . . . oppositions which have been constructed as irreconcilable" including exhausted/tireless, slacker/hard working and self-sacrificing/selfish.[75]

Myer's World War II years also bring to light tensions within masculinity ideals and their intersection with imperialism. The dominant U.S. narrative is replete with stereotypes, which support imperialist violence on the American "frontier" and portray that violence as a heroic white American legacy. Despite his omission of any explicit reference to race in his autobiographical account of his childhood, racism was endemic to rural Ohio, which has a history of killing Native Americans. Myer's correspondence with a Japanese American sergeant exemplifies how notions of masculinity and American imperialism were intertwined in his worldview. The sergeant had suffered a head wound during a fight with a Native American soldier. Myer and the sergeant referred to the wound as an "Indian scalping" and, performing gender, Myer praised the sergeant for his participation in the fistfight.[76]

Controversially, Myer advocated for releasing Japanese American men from WRA camps and enlisting them in the military. Then, he used the soldiers' combat records in a campaign to change Japanese Americans' public image from "enemy aliens" to "all-American G.I. Joes." While Myer pushed the parameters of U.S. national identity, he reinforced the resurgence of war as central to hegemonic masculinity ideology.

Myer was a Presidential appointee and among the "white men in positions of influence and power."[77] These men gained and maintained their positions by performing gender in combative processes such as Congressional hearings. Myer engaged in these processes defending himself and the WRA from the politically powerful white men who sought to undermine him, the WRA and the New Deal's liberal legacy. Whether on the offensive or "on the defense," as he phrased it, Myer performed masculinity in accordance with his and the Brotherhoods' ideology. In his own estimation and that of many other white liberals, his administration of ten concentration camps and his public relations campaign-cum-war were great successes. This supposed success was born out of four years of publicly displaying the Stimsonian leadership characteristics of stoicism, heroism, toughness, optimism, restraint, and resoluteness. These performances and his perceptions of their results validated Myer's masculinity which may be why, as WRA director, he "lost all feeling of insecurity," which had plagued him for decades.[78]

For Myer and professionals participating in projects of domination, culture was wrapped up with science, which they identified as male-centered, unemotional, and intelligent. In autobiographical accounts of his professional roles, Myer does not mention learning from people impacted by his policies or even that learning from them was a possibility. With their university training, planners and policymakers viewed themselves as part of the "community of the competent" who were more knowledgeable than the so-called amateurs on the receiving end of their policies.[79] Chapter 4 focuses on how the liberal ideas of urban and regional planning and related social sciences influenced Myer and WRA policies.[80]

Notes

1 Dillon S. Myer to Mike Masaoka, Dec. 21, 1944, Personal Correspondence 1937–1940, Myer Papers, Truman Library, Independence, MO. Andrew Lind, *Hawaii's Japanese: An Experiment with Democracy* (Princeton, NJ: Princeton University Press, 1946), 158, cited in Ronald Takaki, *Double Victory: A Multicultural History of America in World War II* (Boston, MA: Little, Brown and Co, 2000), 164.

2 Ronald Takaki, *A Different Mirror: A History of Multicultural America* (New York: Back Bay Books, 2008), 347. Dorothy Swaine Thomas with Charles Kikuchi and James Sakoda, *The Salvage* (Berkeley, CA: University of California Press, 1952), 105–106. Dillon S. Myer to Mike Masaoka, Dec. 21, 1944, Personal Correspondence 1937–1940, Myer Papers, Truman Library, Independence, MO. Robert Connell, *Masculinities* (Berkeley: University of California Press, 2005), 213. In September 1942, the Selective Service assigned a 4-C (enemy alien) draft classification to Japanese Americans

infuriating many who understood this policy as part of their wartime persecution. Thomas, Kikuchi and Sakoda place the date of this assignment at June 17, 1942 and note that, in the fall of 1942, the Army modified the policy to recruit Japanese Americans for military intelligence. 1,208 men volunteered from inside WRA camps, thereby, securing their release from the camps.

3 Dillon S. Myer, *An Autobiography of Dillon S. Myer* (Berkeley: University of California, 1970), 365–366.

4 Paul A. Kramer, *The Blood of Government: Race Empire, the United States, and the Philippines* (Chapel Hill, NC: University of North Carolina Press, 2006), 19. Chiara Bottici, "Culture Wars," in *The Encyclopedia of Political Science*, ed. George Thomas Kurian, Vol. 1 (Washington, D.C.: CQ Press, 2011), 370–371, *Gale Virtual Reference Library*, http://link.galegroup.com/apps/doc/CX1671600329/GVRL?u=csus_main&sid=GVRL&x-id=8aed6ea9. Bottici explains, "Culture war refers to a situation of radical conflict between opposite values or worldviews."

5 Carey McWilliams, *Prejudice; Japanese Americans: A Symbol of Racial Intolerance* (Boston, MA: Little, Brown & Co., 1944), 173–174.

6 Charles Vevier, "Yellow Peril," in *Dictionary of American History*, ed. Stanley I. Kutler, Vol. 8 (New York: Charles Scribner's Sons, 2003), 577–578, *Gale Virtual Reference Library*, http://link.galegroup.com/apps/doc/CX3401804636/GVRL?u=csus_main&sid=GVRL&xid=0fd3996. For more on "yellow peril," see Geoffrey S. Smith, "Nativism," in *Encyclopedia of American Foreign Policy*, ed. Richard Dean Burns, Alexander DeConde, and Fredrik Logevall, 2nd ed., Vol. 2 (New York: Charles Scribner's Sons, 2002), 511–527, *Gale Virtual Reference Library*, http://link.galegroup.com/apps/doc/CX3402300093/GVRL?u=csus_main&sid=GVRL&x-id=a597a74c. Mire Koikari, "'Japanese Eyes, American Heart' Politics of Race, Nation, and Masculinity in Japanese American Veterans' WWII Narratives," *Men and Masculinities* 12, no. 5 (2010): 550. Koikari explains that during the war, "the lack of proper masculinity among Japanese American men was a complex issue . . . as they had access to certain, albeit deviant and despised, notions of manliness."

7 Thomas, Kikuchi, and Sadoka, 106. "Memorandum to the President from Attorney General Francis Biddle," Feb. 17, 1942, Franklin D. Roosevelt Presidential Library and Museum, www.fdrlibrary.marist.edu/archives/pdfs/internment.pdf. Robert D. Dean, *Imperial Brotherhood: Gender and the Making of Cold War Foreign Policy* (Amherst, MA: University of Massachusetts, 2003), 38. Walter Lippmann and Westbrook Pegler were influential anti-Japanese American columnists. Dean refers to these contests as "process[es] of inclusion within or exclusion from political power."

8 Dean, 13. George Lipsitz, *The Possessive Investment in Whiteness: How White People Profit from Identity Politics* (Philadelphia, PA: Temple University Press, 2018), vii, ProQuest Ebook Central ProQuest Ebook Central, https://ebookcentral.proquest.com/lib/csus/detail.action?docID=5425334.

9 Myer, *An Autobiography*, 85.

10 Dean, 5, 6. Henry Yu, *Orientals: Migration, Contact, and Exoticism in Modern America* (New York: Oxford University Press, 2001), 32. Benedict Anderson, *Imagined Communities: Reflections on the Origin and Spread of*

Nationalism (London: Verso, 1991). Yu writes, "Almost every Chicago sociologist was from a small rural town, often in what was seen as the West (now the Midwest) of America, and the recurring three-word mantras of their names bespoke white Protestant family heritages."

11 Myer, *An Autobiography*, 1–18. Lipsitz, vii.

12 Paul Theobald and Brianna Theobald, "Education in a Rural Context," in *The Routledge History of Rural America*, ed. Pamela Riney-Kehrberg (New York: Routledge, 2016), 175. According to Theobald and Theobald,

> While [rural schoolchildren's] texts might tell them that the Indian Removal Act sent Cherokees "to a fine country west of the Mississippi," Indians were still "hostile to progress," "uncivilized," and required "quarantine on reservations." . . . To choose sides at a ball game it was often necessary to 'catch a nigger by the toe.'

13 John Modell and Madeline Goodman, "Historical Perspectives," in *At the Threshold: The Developing Adolescent*, ed. S. Shirley Feldman and Glen R. Elliot (Cambridge, MA: Harvard University Press, 1990), quoted in Robert C. Bulman, *Hollywood Goes to High School: Cinema, Schools and American Culture* (New York: Worth Publishers, 2015), 23. "Table 303.70," National Center for Education Statistics, United States Department of Education, Accessed Sept. 3, 2018, https://nces.ed.gov/programs/digest/d16/tables/dt16_303.70.asp. Until the mid-1980s, men were the majority of U.S. students.

14 Steven Brint, "Higher Education," in *Encyclopedia of Sociology*, 2nd ed., Vol. 2 (New York: Macmillan Reference USA, 2001), 1178–1186, *Gale Virtual Reference Library*, http://link.galegroup.com/apps/doc/CX3404400157/GVRL?u=csus_main&sid=GVRL&xid=0482197e. Myer, *An Autobiography*, 1–18, 85.

15 Ibid., 82–83.

16 Ibid., 83, 84.

17 Ibid., 326. Lawrence Feinberg, "18 Women End Cosmos Club's 110-Year Male Era," *Washington Post*, Oct. 12, 1988, www.washingtonpost.com/archive/local/1988/10/12/18-women-end-cosmos-clubs-110-year-male-era/8cc6e3e1-7562-4435-a607-6b1b6b616f27/?utm_term=.76532283b9ae. Dr. McCall co-sponsored Myer with a Dr. Warburton.

18 Donald J. Mrozek, "The Habit of Victory: The American Military and the Cult of Manliness," in *Manliness and Morality: Middle-Class Masculinity in Britain and America, 1800–1940*, ed. J.A. Mangan and James Walvin (Manchester: Manchester University Press, 1987), 222. Jeffrey Ryan Suzik, "'Building Better Men': The CCC Boy and the Changing Social Ideals of Manliness," *Men and Masculinities* 2, no. 2 (1999): 158.

19 Takaki, *A Different*, 7. Gabriel Stepto, ed., "The Ongoing Effort for Inclusion in the Military," in *The African-American Years: Chronologies of American History and Experience* (New York: Charles Scribner's Sons, 2003), 294–311, *Gale Virtual Reference Library*, http://link.galegroup.com/apps/doc/CX3409100025/GVRL?u=csus_main&sid=GVRL&xid=a09f10bf. Lipsitz, 85. Lipsitz explains,

> the [Reagan era] deployment of memories about World War II as a "good war" also rested on nostalgia for a preintegration America, when segregation in the military meant that most war heroes were white,

when de jure and de facto segregation on the home front channeled the fruits and benefits of victory disproportionately to white citizens.

20 Lipsitz, 79. Lipsitz observes, "The possessive investment in whiteness is learned and legitimated in many places that at first glance may seem to have little to do with race. One of those places is warfare."

21 Myer, *An Autobiography*, 160. William Dicke, "Dillon S. Myer, Who Headed War Relocation Agency, Dies," *The New York Times*, 1982, www.nytimes.com/1982/10/25/obituaries/dillon-s-myer-who-headed-war-relocation-agency-dies.html. Suzik, 152, 154, 155–156. J.A. Mangan and James Walvin, *Manliness and Morality: Middle-Class Masculinity in Britain and America, 1800–1940* (Manchester: Manchester University Press, 1987), 6. The Myer's would go on to raise three daughters.

22 Suzik, 152–176.

23 Richard Drinnon, *Keeper of Concentration Camps: Dillon S. Myer and American Racism* (Berkeley, CA: University of California Press, 1987), 44.

24 A second section of the Division of Cooperative Relations and Planning focused on coordinating land use programs further connecting Myer to the then-developing field of urban and regional planning.

25 Drinnon, 18.

26 Milton S. Eisenhower Dies at 85: Served as Advisor to President," *New York Times*, May 3, 1985, www.nytimes.com/1985/05/03/us/milton-s-eisenhower-dies-at-85-served-as-adviser-to-president.html.

27 Myer, *An Autobiography*, 63–64, 126–127. Anthony E. Rotundo, *American Manhood: Transformations in Masculinity from the Revolution to the Modern Era* (New York: Basic Books, 1993), 22. Kramer, *The Blood*, 4. Dillon S. Myer to Glenn K. Rule, Dec. 3, 1935, Personal Correspondence 1934–1935, Myer Papers, Truman Library, Independence, MO. Dicke, "Dillon." See Rotundo regarding the middle-class and the separate spheres doctrine. See Kramer on the impact of imperialism on families. The Department of Agriculture and War Relocation Authority offices were in Washington, D.C. Myer's correspondence shows that, during the 1930s, he lived in Chevy Chase, Maryland.

28 Connell, *Masculinities*, 171. Franzwal et al. 1989, Judith Grant and Peta Tancred, "A Feminist Perspective on State Bureaucracy," in *Gendering Organizational Analysis*, ed. Albert J. Mills and Peta Tancred (Newbury Park, CA: Sage Publications, 1992), 112–128, quoted in Connell, *Masculinities*, 73. Rotundo, 248, 250. In 1930, most typists were women.

29 Connell, *Masculinities*, 171.

30 George W. Kreitler to Dillon S. Myer, Mar. 9, 1938, Personal Correspondence 1937–1940, Myer Papers, Truman Library, Independence, MO. Dillon S. Myer to T.A. Coleman, Oct. 12, 1938, Personal Correspondence 1937–1940, Myer Papers, Truman Library, Independence, MO.

31 Michael S. Kimmel, *Manhood in America: A Cultural History*, 2nd ed. (New York: Oxford University Press, 2006), 60.

32 Suzik, 158, 171, 174.

33 Rotundo, 197.

34 Connell, *Masculinities*, 171. Allan G. Johnson, *The Gender Knot: Unraveling Our Patriarchal*, 3rd ed. (Philadelphia, PA: Temple University Press, 2014), 153.

35 *New York Times*, "Milton." Myer, *An Autobiography*, 183–184. Milton Eisenhower to Dillon S. Myer, July 26, 1946, and Dillon S. Myer to Milton Eisenhower, Aug. 12, 1946, Myer Papers, Truman Library, Independence, MO. Dillon S. Myer, *Uprooted Americans: The Japanese Americans and the War Relocation Authority during World War II* (Tucson, AZ: University of Arizona Press, 1971), 185.

36 Dillon S. Myer to Russel Lord, July 14, 1942, Personal Correspondence 1941–1942, Myer Papers, Truman Library, Independence, MO.

37 Connell, *Masculinities*, 213.

38 Christina Jarvis, *The Male Body at War: American Masculinity during World War II* (DeKalb, NC: Northern Illinois University Press, 2004), 128, quoted in Aaron Belkin, *Bring Me Men: Military Masculinity and the Benign Façade of American Empire, 1898–2001* (New York: Columbia University Press, 2012), 52.

39 Michael John Wallinger, *Dispersal of the Japanese American: Rhetorical Strategies of the War Relocation Authority, 1942–1945* (Ph.D. diss., University of Oregon 1975), 383–384. Greg Robinson, *By Order of the President: FDR and the Internment of Japanese Americans* (Cambridge, MA: Harvard University Press, 2001), 179. According to Wallinger, Myer's goal of en masse indefinite leave necessitated "an able and imaginative rhetorical counterforce to the voices of repression and racism."

40 Dean, 7, 169–170. Myer, *An Autobiography*, 106.

41 Dean, 10. "About Henry L. Stimson," Stimson Center, Accessed Sept. 3, 2018, www.stimson.org/content/about-henry-l-stimson. Freidel and Sidey, "Dwight D. Eisenhower." Henry L. Stimson (1867–1950) was a lawyer and statesman who served four U.S. presidents.

42 Rachel Sady to Edward Spicer, June 30, 1945, Rachel Sady Folder, Spicer Papers, University of Arizona, Tucson.

43 J.Y. Smith, "Rexford Tugwell, Adviser in FDR's 'Brains Trust,' Dies," *Washington Post*, July 25, 1979, www.washingtonpost.com/archive/local/1979/07/25/rexford-tugwell-adviser-in-fdrs-brains-trust-dies/68a9b1c6-d8c3-44f7-b7d0-2599bada50c4/?noredirect=on&utm_term=.fd423246b388.

44 Hearings Before A Subcommittee on Military Affairs of the United States Senate–78th Congress, First Session on Jan. 20, 27 and 28 1943. S. 444 p. 60, WRA Memoranda and Reports 1943–1946, Myer Papers, Truman Library, Independence, MO. "Letter, Sen. Harley M. Kilgore to President Roosevelt," Feb. 19, 1942, Franklin D. Roosevelt Presidential Library and Museum, www.fdrlibrary.marist.edu/archives/pdfs/internment.pdf. Robinson, 182–183. "Myer Sees Fear Barrier to Japs," n.d., John A. Rademaker, Spicer Papers, University of Arizona, Tucson. The White House received Senator Kilgore's letter the day after FDR signed EO 9066. Democratic Senator Joseph C. O'Mahoney of Wyoming called upon the U.S. Ambassador to Japan to discuss if there was anything inherently mistrustful about Japanese and, therefore, Japanese Americans. A newspaper heading, "Myer Sees Fear Barrier to Japs," exemplifies how Myer publicized the views that racist feelings needed to be dispelled with knowledge and that Japanese Americans were not inherently frightening.

45 Dillon S. Myer to O.G. Anderson, July 16, 1943, Personal Correspondence 1943–1944, Myer Papers, Truman Library, Independence, MO.

46 Robinson, 192. Brian Hayashi, *Democratizing the Enemy* (Princeton, NJ: Princeton University Press, 2004), 129. Takaki, *A Different*, 347. Myer, *Uprooted Americans*, 61. In the of fall 1942, the Japanese American Citizen League held a conference in Salt Lake City where chapter leaders passed a resolution endorsing the restoration of the drafting of Japanese Americans.

47 Aaron Belkin, *Bring Me Men: Military Masculinity and the Benign Façade of American Empire, 1898–2001* (New York: Columbia University Press, 2012), 3–4.

48 Dean, 50. Myer, *An Autobiography*, 80–82. Hearings Before A Subcommittee on Military Affairs of the United States Senate–78th Congress, First Session on Jan. 20, 27 and 28 1943. S. 444 p. 54–55, WRA Memoranda and Reports 1943–1946, Myer Papers, Truman Library, Independence, MO. Robert N. Bellah, Richard Madsen, William M. Sullivan, Ann Swindler, and Steven M. Tipton, *Habits of the Heart: Individualism and Commitment in American Life* (New York: Harper and Row), 1985, cited in Bulman, 21. Koikari, 552. Dean explains that, "For a politically ambitious self-made man, the ordeals and ritual tests of manhood were less rigidly patterned and more contingent upon self-direction than those of the patrician; nonetheless, a demonstration of military valor was just as crucial." Myer ambitiousness fits the understanding of middle-class posited by Robert Bellah and his co-authors according to which members of the middle-class strive for material comforts and make a conscious effort to move up in social status.

49 Drinnon, 57.

50 Hearings Before A Subcommittee on Military Affairs of the United States Senate–78th Congress, First Session on Jan. 20, 27 and 28 1943. S. 444 p. 54–55, WRA Memoranda and Reports 1943–1946, Myer Papers, Truman Library, Independence, MO.

51 Ibid., John Radzilowski, "Hajiro, Barney F.," in *Asian and Pacific Islander Americans*, ed. Gary Y. Okihiro, Great Lives from History, Vol. 1 (Ipswich, MA: Salem Press, 2013), 246–247, *Gale Virtual Reference Library*, http://link.galegroup.com/apps/doc/CX2075200146/GVRL?u=csus_main&sid=GVRL&xid=a20d192f. This change of policy was due to U.S. military's interest in using Japanese American soldiers to counter Japanese propaganda, as well as to civil liberties groups' advocacy and Myer's efforts.

52 Christina Jarvis, *The Male Body at War: American Masculinity during World War II* (DeKalb, IL: Northern Illinois University Press, 2004), 4–5, quoted in Belkin, 36.

53 Kramer, *The Blood*, 4. Kramer explains, race's "gradations of humanity would also facilitate ultimate forms of exclusion: the extreme violence upon which those [imperial] states would often be constructed."

54 Dillon S. Myer to Mike Masaoka, Dec. 21, 1944, Myer Papers, Truman Library, Independence, MO.

55 Thomas, Kikuchi, and Sakoda, 107–108.

56 Dillon S. Myer to Joe Kanazawa, n.d., Personal Correspondence 1943–1944, Dillon S. Myer Papers, Truman Library, Independence, MO.

57 Stanley I. Thangaraj, *Desi Hoop Dreams: Pickup Basketball and the Making of Asian American Masculinity* (New York: New York University Press, 2015), 24.

58 Ibid., 203. Kathy E. Ferguson and Phyllis Turnbull, *Oh, Say, Can You See? The Semiotics of the Military in Hawai'i* (Minneapolis: University of

Minnesota Press, 1999), 155–198. Koikari, 549. Japanese American men had diverse reasons for joining the military. Some were motivated by patriotism. Some wanted to get out of the camps, and some saw enlisting as a strategy which would gain themselves and their families the right to stay in the United States.

59 Dillon S. Myer to O.G. Anderson, July 16, 1943, Personal Correspondence 1943–1944, Myer Papers, Truman Library, Independence, MO.

60 Ibid.

61 Ronald Takaki, *Hiroshima: Why America Dropped the Atomic Bomb* (Boston, MA: Little, Brown, and Co., 1995), 109–120. Brenda M. Boyle, *Masculinity in Vietnam War Narratives: A Critical Study of Fiction, Films and Nonfiction Writings* (Jefferson, NC: McFarland & Company, 2009), 144–164, quoted in Belkin, 2.

62 Myer, *An Autobiography*, 365–366.

63 Myer, *An Autobiography*. Myer, *Uprooted Americans*. Takaki, *Hiroshima*, 9.

64 Ibid.

65 Joseph H. Pleck, *Myth of Masculinity* (Cambridge, MA: MIT Press, 1981), 140.

66 Dean, 5.

67 Myer, *An Autobiography*, 365–366.

68 Ibid., 106, 195. Robinson, 178. Myer notes that the exceptions to his sound sleeping were during November and December 1942 when there was unrest in the Poston and Manzanar camps.

69 Myer, *An Autobiography*, 87, 146–147, 365–366.

70 Ibid., 146–147.

71 Ibid.

72 Ibid., 147–148.

73 Thangaraj, 23.

74 Dean, 6, 52, 183.

75 Belkin, 4–5.

76 Drinnon, 13. Ben Kuroki to Dillon S. Myer, Aug. 26, 1945, and Dillon S. Myer to Ben Kuroki, Oct. 5, 1945, Personal Correspondence 1945, Myer Papers, Truman Library, Independence, MO.

77 Takaki, *Hiroshima*, 8–9.

78 Connell, *Masculinities*, 75. Tony Badger, "New Deal," in *Encyclopedia of the Great Depression*, ed. Robert S. McElvaine, Vol. 2 (New York: Macmillan Reference USA, 2004), 701–711, *Gale Virtual Reference Library*, http://link.galegroup.com/apps/doc/CX3404500395/GVRL?u=csus_main&sid=GVRL&xid=61d8392b. Myer, *An Autobiography*, 365–366.

79 Michael Hibbard, "Public Epistemologies and Policy Planning: The Case of American Indian Policy," (Ph.D. diss., University of California Los Angeles, 1980), 44. Hibbard borrows "community of the competent" from Francis E. Abbot.

80 Ibid., Jane Jacobs, *The Death and Life of Great American Cities* (New York: Vintage Books, 1992), 6, 13. In her classic book, first published in 1961, Jacobs strongly critiques the "the expert knows best" paradigm and its impact. A notable exception to the top-down flow of information was the ethnographic data used to subvert the will of the population under administration.

Photo 4 Phil Hara, WRA Employee Incarcerated in Manzanar, in Front of the Work-Offer Board for Long and Short-Term Employment Outside of the Camp, 1943.

Source: Adams, Ansel, photographer. *Corporal Jimmie Shohara's ribbons, Manzanar Relocation Center / photograph by Ansel Adams.* California Manzanar, 1943. Photograph. https://www.loc.gov/item/2002695319/.

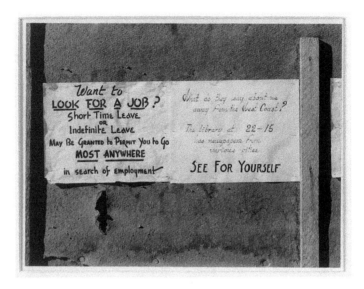

Photo 5 Work-Offer Board Detail, WRA Manzanar Camp, 1943.

Source: Adams, Ansel, photographer. *Detail of work-offer board, Manzanar Relocation Center / photograph by Ansel Adams.* California Manzanar, 1943. Photograph. https://www.loc.gov/item/2002695982/.

Photo 6 Packing for "Indefinite Leave," WRA Manzanar Camp, 1943.

Source: Adams, Ansel, photographer. *Relocation: Packing Up, Manzanar Relocation Center / photograph by Ansel Adams.* California Manzanar, 1943. Photograph. https://www.loc.gov/item/2002695977/.

Photo 7 Goodbyes as Friends and Family Separate, 1, WRA Manzanar Camp, 1943.

Source: Adams, Ansel, photographer. *Relocation good-byes, Manzanar Relocation Center / photograph by Ansel Adams.* California Manzanar, 1943. Photograph. https://www.loc.gov/item/20017404628/.

Photo 8 Goodbyes as Friends and Family Separate, 2, WRA Manzanar
      Camp, 1943.

4 Forced migration "the American Way"

Race and the War Relocation Authority

In June 1943, War Relocation Authority (WRA) director, Dillon S. Myer, addressed the U.S. public via "The March of Time," *Time* magazine's series of short films on controversial topics, which played along with newsreels in movie theaters across the country. Myer pointedly challenged his compatriots, "Let's not deal with the problem as Hitler would handle it under his Nazi regime, or as Tojo would deal with it in Japan. Let's do it in the American way."[1] The "problem" to which he was referring was the federal government's imprisonment of Japanese Americans in WRA concentration camps. Myer wanted to persuade the American masses that the solution needed to reflect the ideal of equality and contrast with Germany and Japan's contemporary persecution of racialized groups. His words hit at the heart of national identity and wartime patriotism while, also, reflecting contemporary shifts in social science. The WRA's policies and politics evinced developments in social scientists' understandings of race and nation as much as they did the masculinity ideologies discussed in Chapter 3.

During World War II, Germany committed genocide against Jews and the Japanese military committed horrific violence against civilians. While all three nations were imperialist, U.S. propaganda portrayed the United States as a nation of equality. This narrative countered Japan's depiction of itself as the challenger of U.S. oppression of nonwhites. Also, American propaganda, including that of the WRA, emphasized the United States' differences from Germany in order to dissociate the two countries. The National Socialists' ideology reminded the world, much of which was under Western domination, that Hitler's ideas were not categorically different from those which leaders of other European and European-derived nations had espoused.

As Euro-American nations, the United States and Germany shared histories and cultures including white supremacist ideologies, genocidal imperialism, and racist exploitation. Because of Germany's military successes in Europe, the Allies entered World War II. Countering white supremacy was not their motivation for war with Germany. In fact, mobilizing the world against the Axis powers included attempting to cleanse the Allies' image of white supremacy as it was at the core of the modern French, British, and U.S. nations. As the WRA exemplified, the U.S. government continued to oppress nonwhites while representing the nation as culturally superior to the Axis powers and, especially, distinct from the contemporary German regime. Attentive to global optics, the Roosevelt administration was eager to show that its imprisonment of Japanese Americans did not resemble the Nazi's incarceration of Jews.

Politicians and government officials used social scientists' studies of WRA camps to counter Japan's claims that the United States was waging a race war. By February 1943, President Roosevelt and some of his Cabinet members were anxious for major changes in the WRA to minimize fuel for Japanese propaganda.[2] They wanted to manage their global optics and solve the "Japanese problem" by releasing nuclear families and individuals. Nuclear family and individual release complemented the New Deal ideology that nonwhites would assimilate if given an environment that immersed them in whiteness. It also appeased those who wanted to prevent Japanese Americans from living outside of the camps in large groups and who perceived Japanese Americans as the yellow peril.

During World War II, Japanese Americans contested government policies in four cases, which went to the U.S. Supreme Court. *Ex parte Endo v. United States* was the case that challenged the WRA's policy of requiring "loyal" Japanese Americans to apply for indefinite leave and subject themselves to monitoring after they left the camps. This direct challenge to one of the WRA's main roles is probably why the agency's lawyers found *Endo* particularly threatening.[3] WRA solicitor Philip Glick offered to release Endo with the provision that she would not be allowed to return to California in accordance with Public Proclamation No. 1. Endo refused this offer and stayed in WRA camps until the U.S. Supreme Court reached its decision on her case two years later.[4]

Immediately prior to World War II, U.S. domestic policies toward nonwhites had begun to improve with the New Deals for Native Americans and African Americans. For Myer and his staff, Japanese Americans' indefinite leave out of the camps exemplified "the American way" and built on the New Deal legacy of applying city and regional planning (planning), sociology, and anthropology to nonwhites. Japanese Americans, however, experienced indefinite leave as a second forced migration or as relief from their original forced migration away from the West Coast and into the camps.

Many immigrants resented the mandatory "loyalty" examinations and that, at first, they were not eligible for indefinite leave. Some did not want to be released because they feared violent racists and because, with the original forced migration, they had lost their livelihoods. Robinson explains, "They objected to a procedure they feared was designed to push them out of the camps and cast them adrift." At first, Question 28 of the loyalty exam required immigrants to renounce their Japanese citizenship, which would have left them stateless. Ineligible for U.S. citizenship because of the 1790 naturalization law, for these immigrants, their Japanese citizenship was their only citizenship. After complaints, the WRA changed Question 28 to ask immigrants to "abide" by U.S. laws. The entire process heightened anger and fear inside the concentration camps.[5]

As Warwick Anderson describes the Philippines and Puerto Rico, the WRA camps were "borderlands where many 'experts' were experimenting with national bodies . . ."[6] The WRA "experimented" with the U.S. national body. Myer wanted to enlarge it to include Japanese Americans without fundamentally changing its dominant culture.[7]

Reform and control

In the late 1800s and early 1900s, East Coast cities and Chicago also functioned as "borderlands" where "'experts'" experimented with "national bodies." These cities became the homes of the highest numbers of impoverished immigrants to arrive to the United States since the Irish had escaped the 1840s potato famine. In addition to those who sought to survive poverty, there were many Jewish refugees fleeing the pogroms of Eastern Europe.[8]

Exploited in the industrial revolution, many of these poor urbanites were drawn to labor unions, which many middle and upper-class Americans equated with national insecurity and class warfare. Encouraged by the idea of environmental determinism and galvanized during the industrial depression and labor radicalism of the 1890s, middle-class reformers sought to overhaul slum housing and address issues such as sanitation and overcrowding. Proponents of environmental determinism, the idea that controlling the physical environment can directly impact the behavior of people in that environment, reformers believed that improving slum housing and poor neighborhoods would lead to parallel and positive changes in the residents.[9]

For the urban reformers, controlling slum residents' political and social behavior went hand in hand with ameliorating housing conditions. They believed that poor housing led to a low quality of life and a lack of morals and that, without their reforms, the European immigrants and their children would degrade the nation and not assimilate.[10] The predominantly Protestant white reformers considered the newly arrived Southern and Eastern Europeans, many of whom were Catholics and Jews, as their cultural, not only their class, inferiors. Similarly, Myer and other white liberals would attempt to reform Japanese Americans whom they believed to be culturally inferior and in need of assimilation.

During Myer's career as well as that of the early reformers, city and regional planning and other professionals were overwhelmingly white, male and bourgeois, but white, bourgeois women volunteers, like early female doctors and lawyers, transgressed the doctrine of separate gender spheres. White middle-class women created niches within the housing reform movement where they occupied recognized positions in the public sphere while maintaining their gendered roles as physical and moral caretakers. Whether male, female, professional or volunteer, planners approached social reform from a top-down perspective as would the New Deal-dominated WRA. The U.S. government's forced removal of Japanese Americans followed and coincided with the biggest growth period of city and regional planning in U.S. history as the Roosevelt administration implemented planning on a large scale in the 1930s and as a defense strategy during World War II.[11]

Daniel Burnham, whose career flourished during the housing reform era, authored celebrated city plans including the Chicago Plan of 1909, the San Francisco Plan of 1905, and the Philippine Plan of 1905, which was part of U.S. imperialist rule of the Philippine Islands. Burnham declared, "Make no small plans!"[12] This declaration epitomized the idea that an all-encompassing, singular, and monolithic plan developed by a single professional or small group of professionals should dominate urban growth and where, how, and with whom city residents should live, work, and recreate.

A few decades after early housing reform's peak and Burnham's city plans, the United States Department of Agriculture (USDA) played a center role in the Great Depression's New Deal. A key figure of social reform planning, Rexford Tugwell, was an original member of President Roosevelt's brain trust, Assistant Secretary of Agriculture (1933–1934), and Undersecretary of Agriculture (1934–1935). He headed several agencies including the Resettlement Administration and the Agricultural Adjustment Administration.[13]

Tugwell was born in a small town in New York state in 1891, which was the same year that Myer was born in rural Ohio. The son of a prosperous cattle farmer, he attended the University of Pennsylvania's Wharton School of Finance and Commerce during the years that Myer studied at the Ohio State University. Tugwell stayed on at the University of Pennsylvania earning his master's and doctoral degrees. After ten years on Columbia University's faculty, he entered the Bourgeois Brotherhood when a Columbia colleague ushered him in recruiting him to join FDR's brain trust and presidential campaign. Once Roosevelt was inaugurated, Tugwell yielded influence well beyond his official titles. As housing reformers had on a smaller scale, Tugwell viewed himself and other planners as leaders who would save the nation.[14] His ambitions echoed Burham's declaration, "Make no small plans!"

While some accused him of being a socialist, Tugwell described himself as a liberal. Paradigms of social science, including planning, such as those of social hierarchies, top-down methodology, and white cultural superiority were part of Myer's professional culture and the liberal New Deal. Myer worked under Tugwell at the USDA where social scientists and government bureaucrats collaborated in their administration of people and land. During the New Deal, a paternalistic style characterized Myer's work at the Agricultural Adjustment Administration where he implemented policies at the state level, which Tugwell had formulated at the federal level.[15]

As one who contributed to policies which impacted Americans and American imperialism, Tugwell theorized about differences among human beings. A modern social scientist, he viewed thinking "effectively" as the sign of superior "man" and viewed some people as "very close to the level of their animal relatives in forethought and the management of their lives. . ."[16] Comparing people to animals may have reflected a pseudo-scientific rationale for imperialism or that Tugwell believed that it was through education that he and other Bourgeois Brothers gained their "higher" reasoning abilities. Whether he believed in innate "blood of government" or the intellectual preparedness to govern, Tugwell was a classic imperialist whose worldview resembled that of his British counterparts.[17]

During World War II, Tugwell served as the governor of Puerto Rico for which he moved from Washington, D.C., a place of people whom he considered superior, to a place where people were, from his perspective, much closer to their "animal relatives." Like many imperialist administrators, Tugwell subscribed to an idea that Anderson aptly captures: "Only bourgeois white males were truly qualified to reach the endpoint of civilization . . ."[18] While Myer rejected the idea of innate racial superiority, he shared Tugwell's belief in white cultural superiority. During World War II, Myer and his staff governed people whom they considered culturally inferior. For WRA business trips in remote and supposedly culturally inferior parts of the United States, they left Washington, D.C., and other supposedly superior cities.

The director during the WRA's first months, Milton Eisenhower had staffed the WRA with former USDA employees closely connecting the agency to Tugwell and city and regional planning. Planning theories, concepts, and methods as well as those from the related fields of applied anthropology and sociology dominated WRA epistemology. Myer's ambitions as WRA director echoed the New Deal during which no goal was too big for federal policymakers.[19]

Raw deals and New Deals

New Deal social science practices, which targeted Native Americans and African Americans, reemerged in Japanese Americans' World War II human rights violations. For African Americans, the New Deal began as a "Raw Deal," because of the FDR administration's racism and its efforts to please Southern Democrats. The South controlled the majority of leadership in every New Deal Congress, and Southern Congressmen, industrial associations, local unions, and farm lobbies exploited African Americans' vulnerability.[20] This collaboration of regional political elites, agriculture interests, and lobbyists resembles that of the West Coast, which would exploit Japanese American vulnerability in the 1940s.

Disguised in euphemistic phrases such as the Tennessee Valley Authority director's "grassroots democracy" and U.S. Department of Agriculture Secretary Henry Wallace's "hierarchy of New England town meeting," early New Deal planning in rural agriculture dramatically decreased the quality of life for thousands of African Americans who lost their land, faced starvation, and were forced to migrate north.[21] This history directly connects planning projects like the Tennessee Valley Authority to the New Deal violations of African Americans' rights and the World War II violations of Japanese Americans' rights.

After 1936, with FDR's reelection and the Second New Deal, Tugwell and other liberals, including Eleanor Roosevelt and Harold Ickes, managed to prevail in policies which positively impacted African Americans while maintaining white domination. By the late 1930s, the New Deal for African Americans included jobs and segregated housing in the Public Works Administration, the Housing

Authority, and other federal agencies. The government addressed some of African Americans' needs and acknowledged some of their historical contributions to the nation. The New Deal fundamentally changed Americans' relationship to their government and African Americans were no exception, yet the liberal policies were simultaneously oppressive and progressive.[22]

The effort to avoid appearing racist before the international community further liberalized policies and contributed to the New Deal's domestic criticism. The aim of contrasting the United States' treatment of African Americans with Germany and Italy's contemporary violence against nonwhites conflicted with a U.S. government plagued by racists. For example, Texas Congressman Martin Dies criticized the federal government's concern for African Americans as "communist" and "subversive."[23] Four years later, Dies and his Sub-Committee on Un-American Activities brought Myer before them to defend WRA policies.

Like the African American New Deal, the Native American New Deal was a substantial change in federal government policy, which also reinforced a racist hierarchy. These policies recognized indigenous cultures and social organizations more than previous policies had. Rather than equating modernization with cultural and economic assimilation, BIA "Chief" John Collier's understanding of assimilation emphasized economics.[24] Collier hoped that the 1934 Indian Reorganization Act (IRA) would codify his vision.

Although Collier wanted the IRA to end Native American assimilation and provide for economic rehabilitation, the IRA's final form did not go far toward implementing his vision. Nonetheless, many white Americans objected to its lack of emphasis on cultural assimilation. As they did African American New Deal policies, critics labeled the IRA as "communist." Flora Warren Seymour, a former member of the Board of Indian Commissioners, criticized the IRA as the FDR administration's most extreme "communistic" experiment, and an article about the legislation in the *New York Herald Tribune* appeared under the title, "Commissioner of Indian Affairs Urges Tribesmen to Accept Soviet Type Rule." Collier's attempt to isolate modernity from white culture clashed with contemporary policy paradigms including the assimilationist paradigm, which would dominate the WRA.[25]

In December 1935, after agricultural scientists had met with Navajo resistance to a sheep reduction program, USDA Secretary Wallace approved Collier's proposal to create a social science unit within the Soil Conservation Service (SCS) to work with the BIA. Myer was part of this institutional culture as he worked for the SCS in 1935. In 1936, the USDA hired a sociologist, Eshrev Shevky, onto the sheep reduction project. Anthropologists Burleigh Gardner, Sol Kimball, and John Provinse joined thereafter taking their functionalist anthropologic training to the SCS. As Lawrence Kelly explains, functionalism "described how the culture worked" and "functionalists were interested in those aspects of a society which were also of most interest to government planners: land and property concepts, social and political organization, kinship patterns, native law, status systems."[26]

Shevky, Garder, Kimball, and Provinse were part of a lineage of social scientists who served imperial powers. They viewed functionalism as a reform tool to help the Navajo.[27] Like anthropologists and planners before them and as the WRA would a few years later, they did not distinguish between social control and social reform.

In 1938, Provinse and Kimball investigated Navajo social organization and studied their "'land use community.'" By working within the Navajo cultural framework and with indigenous leaders, they planned to implement policies which Navajo people were resisting. Whereas traditional agriculturalists had not considered indigenous cultures, these social scientists attempted to communicate with Navajo on Navajo cultural terms. Provinse attempted to apply knowledge of a culture to implement policies against people's wills. Along with other scholars and officials, he and his colleagues assumed that the government and subordinated groups had the same interests. Provinse, Kimball, and Gardner were among the New Dealers who would find employment at the WRA. For example, Provinse became the WRA Chief of Community Management.[28]

Contrasting the WRA and the BIA with the federal government's previous exploitation and neglect of nonwhites, liberals viewed culturally specific programs as progress. In his 1943 book, *Brothers Under the Skin*, Carey McWilliams urged other agencies to follow the BIA in employing social scientists. During the Great Depression and in the postwar years, McWilliams worked as a planner and, during World War II, he headed California's Division of Immigration and Housing. On February 10, 1942, McWilliams wrote about a plan to incarcerate Japanese Americans then release them temporarily when agribusiness wanted laborers. Before FDR created the WRA, McWilliams had wired the U.S. Attorney General suggesting the establishment of an "Alien Control Authority." He, like many culture and policymakers, considered Japanese Americans dangerously concentrated although, in 1941, they were only 1 percent of California's population.[29]

McWilliams and Myer communicated during the war, and the indirect administrative approach which McWilliams outlines in *Brothers Under the Skin* inspired Myer. In tune with McWilliams' approach and connecting planning and the WRA, after working with the Soil Conservation Service and the BIA, Provinse moved to Washington, D.C. where he worked at the USDA's Resettlement Administration. In Washington, D.C., he and his colleagues designed the Culture of a Contemporary Rural Community project by producing studies, which policymakers and planners used in designing land use programs.[30]

Meanwhile, social scientists increasingly looked to environmental, instead of biological, explanations of whites' prejudices and nonwhites' supposedly inferior cultures. Anderson states that in the 1920s and 1930s, "Racial typologies became increasingly unstable and unsatisfying" and "the texture of ideas about race, culture, and environment proved ever more friable."[31] Discussing Chicago sociologist Robert Park, Sitkoff writes,

> In the 1920s, even critical anti-white supremacist scholar, Robert Park, described racial prejudice as "an instinctive factor." He believed racism was largely immune to correction by interracial contact or education, but by the end of the thirties, Park shared most sociologists' view that prejudice was not innate.[32]

Park exemplifies how, by World War II, liberal social scientists had revamped theories on racism and were motivated to increase interracial contact in order to reduce prejudice.

Between liberals' developments and the Nazi's stigmatization of the idea of white biological superiority, beginning in the 1940s, social explanations of racism started to predominate in the United States. Whereas liberal public officials and social scientists had struggled to respond to the idea of an innate white superiority, this paradigm shift led to more opportunities for them to engage in public policy. As the shift from biological theories to social theories took place without debunking the myth of whites' cultural superiority, for many nonwhites, forced assimilation became the modern-day white supremacy.[33] In other words, assimilationist programs were liberal manifestations of white supremacy and not antiracist or nonracist.

The Japanese American New Deal

Navy Lieutenant Commander Alexander Leighton was the first to undertake social science research for the WRA. He worked on behalf of the WRA, the Navy, and the Bureau of Indian Affairs in a WRA camp located on BIA-operated land. Leighton's research resulted in a book and a coauthored article.[34]

Japanese American responses to WRA policies included strikes, resistance to indefinite leave, riots, and physical assaults on Japanese Americans whom others believed to be WRA collaborators. After the December 1942 unrest in the Poston and Manzanar camps, Myer hired social scientists as "community analysts" to work in all WRA camps and at WRA headquarters. He made these liberal scholars his instrumental source of information because he wanted to keep the WRA a civilian New Deal-like agency. As Myer's key epistemological choice, the ethnographers' specialization in culture had a direct impact on policy. Applying ethnographic data to subvert Japanese Americans' will and, previously, that of Navajo, diverged from the top-down flow of information, which had shaped earlier social reform policy.[35]

Using culture to socially control Japanese Americans bolstered the WRA's propaganda campaign. If the government had resorted to force as a primary tool, white Americans, the yellow peril propaganda press, and the military could have interpreted that violence as further indication that Japanese Americans were national security threats. Ethnographers' euphemistic descriptions contributed to the WRA-cultivated image of Japanese Americans, denied the reality of their human rights violations, and fed the myth of American exceptionalism. Examples of these euphemisms include community analyst Marvin Opler referring to a camp as a "colony" and to Japanese American prisoners as "colonists."[36]

In a 1943 letter, community analyst John Rademaker wrote that he accepted his WRA position, so he could help people. In the patronizing vein of colonial administrators and social reformers, Myer and his researchers thought they were helping Japanese Americans by maximizing indirect, manipulative tactics. The manipulation was such that Opler suspected that administrators attempted to coerce dentists and doctors to take indefinite leave by appointing prejudiced white supervisors in clinics.[37]

Although in confidential letters, Myer had argued for an early rescission of the exclusion orders, publicly he and the WRA attorneys defended the government's policies. In a July 1944 statement before the House Sub-committee on Un-American Activities, Myer argued that the indefinite leave policy was constitutional:

> It is the position of the War Relocation Authority that its Leave Regulations are essential to the legal validity of the evacuation and relocation program. . . the evacuation was within the constitutional power of the National Government. . . in the interest of military necessity. . .[38]

For Myer, indefinite leave was an attainable and defendable option, because it complemented his ideas about assimilation, Americanization, and social reform.

As in the Native American New Deal, Provinse and other WRA social scientists applied a functionalist framework to reform. Orin Starn details how structural functionalism supported imperialist projects and influenced WRA research:

> Malinowski's . . . work training colonial administrators at the London School of Economics provided an early example of anthropology's practical uses. The impact of Radcliffe-Brown, who lectured at the University of Chicago from 1931 to 1937 . . . had an enormous influence on the prewar generation of graduate students and young professors . . . from which the majority of the WRA ethnographers were drawn.[39]

The theoretical contribution of structural functionalism coupled with the practical example of colonial administration fit Myer's agenda. As a result, the dual legacy of Malinowski's training of administrators and Radcliffe-Brown's appointment at the University of Chicago impacted the WRA.[40]

Radcliffe-Brown's instruction at the University of Chicago coincided with the emergence of that university's framework for studying Asian Americans. Influenced by Chicago Sociology, social scientists who strove to "improve" "race relations" focused on the ways in which Japanese and other Asian Americans differed from the white middle class. They regarded external cultural traits such as dress and hairstyle, which resembled those of white Americans as proof of assimilation. In their efforts to increase assimilation, WRA social scientists urged that indefinite leave curriculum include table manners and dress.[41]

Henry Yu explains that geography was fundamental to Chicago sociologists' understanding of race and culture as

> they visualized such differences in the forms of maps and other spatial diagrams. Such spatial representation depended on an imagined link that connected the physical spaces of Chinatowns or Japantowns in the United States with the mythical space of the Orient somewhere in Asia.[42]

The government's removal of Japanese Americans from the West Coast was akin to cleansing that region of Orientalized spaces.

Robert Park developed the race relations cycle, a concept that connects "space" and "race," embedding "the social interactions of 'race' and 'culture' into the very physical structure of America."[43] According to the race relations cycle, once a group immigrated, its assimilation into the established group was inevitable. The groups' physical proximity would irreversibly lead to the immigrant group assimilating the established group's culture to the extent that the two would eventually no longer be distinct. According to this theory, immigrants' cultures change and that of the dominant group remains static.[44]

WRA policy fit into the social scientists' theorization about the world into binaries like traditional versus modern and rural versus urban. By moving Japanese Americans from rural to urban, from traditional to modern, from the Old World to the New World, indefinite leave became a way for Myer to participate in these social transformations on a mass scale.[45] As Myer did not doubt the positive value of these changes on the nation or on his own life, he was certain that they would benefit Japanese Americans.

Social scientists who had worked with Navajo "natural leaders" sought to identify leaders among Japanese Americans. These efforts mirrored the ethnographers' training in which they learned to gain key informants' collaboration. In June 1943, Opler reported what he considered success in the Tule Lake camp. Having analyzed the population, he selected his Japanese American staff "at the advice of leading colonists." Pleased that Japanese Americans gathered at the community analysts' offices, Opler wrote to a colleague: "I can assure you that we are definitely 'in' with the colony . . ."[46]

Community analysts viewed noncompliant Japanese Americans as outliers and referred to them as "squeaks" in need of "lubrication" or, to use Leighton's terminology, as suffering from a "disease of society."[47] As with the Navajo, social scientists held that the subordinated group and the government shared goals. Regarding tension among Japanese Americans as a type of noncompliance, they believed that Japanese Americans would gladly change their behavior once social scientists pointed out the tensions' causes.[48]

Robert Redfield was the University of Chicago's Dean of Social Sciences and a WRA consultant. In April 1943, he thanked Myer for having attended a seminar earlier that year and conveyed Park's assessment of the seminar as the university's best yet on "race relations." Redfield shared that Park was "greatly impressed by the realistic and penetrating analysis which the [War Relocation] Authority officers had given to their problem" and considered the WRA a source of "new pride in his country."[49]

That same month, in the Jerome, Arkansas, camp, community analyst Edgar McVoy reported a "squeak." Many Japanese Americans were resisting indefinite leave, because they understood it as another forced migration. Some people were spreading stories about others' negative experiences on the outside. As a form of "lubrication," McVoy suggested that the WRA provide more support to those being released and generate more pro-leave propaganda.[50] On June 12, 1943, frustrated by the slow leave rate, Myer instructed his staff to make indefinite leave their highest priority. That month, he issued a memo ordering that pro-leave materials be sent to the camps and that staff disseminate the materials face-to-face as well as via pamphlets.[51]

In tandem with social scientists, the government hired celebrated photographers, Ansel Adams and Dorothea Lange, and a little-known portrait photographer from Los Angeles, Toyo Miyatake, who was incarcerated in the Manzanar camp. Ralph Merritt, the Manzanar director and Adams' friend, instructed Adams to not include barbed wire, armed guards, or guard towers in his photographs. The WRA authorized Adams' exhibit, which he published as a book, *Born Free and Equal*, in 1944. *Born Free and Equal* was reviewed favorably and made the *San Francisco Chronicle*'s bestseller lists for March and April 1945.[52]

Instead of documenting a massive human rights violation, as Elena Tajima Creef describes them, Adams' photographs depict "all-Americans" ". . . 'solid,' 'cheerful,' and thoroughly 'clean' men, women and children." Creef discusses the photographs as "remarkable for the complex ways in which they each attempted to reinscribe the Japanese American face and body with visible signs of American citizenship, loyalty and heroism."[53] Adams' photographs complemented the social scientists' research and the role assigned to Japanese Americans soldiers. The WRA used the photographs, research, and soldiers to portray Japanese Americans as "real" Americans and support propaganda, which portrayed the United States as culturally superior to the Axis powers.[54] Depicting Japanese Americans as "real" Americans served the WRA agenda by paving the way for positive receptions of Japanese Americans outside of the camps. It also countered Japanese propaganda that nonwhites suffered from white rule and needed Japan to come to their aid.

In Administrative Instruction Number 96, Myer emphasized that indefinite leave into "normal" American life was the WRA's primary concern: "The implementation of the policy must be achieved by staff and prisoners alike. For example, teachers are to give relocation [leave] problems to schoolchildren and to include it in curriculum for night school." Also, Myer instructed, "Project artists and art classes to translate [leave] statistical material into pictograph charts."[55] According to him, Japanese Americans were to develop opinions favorable to indefinite leave, digest curriculum about it, and contribute their talents to implementing it.

Myer's goal of using indefinite leave to disperse Japanese Americans in the Midwest and East Coast reflected the perception that Japanese Americans had too densely populated the West Coast before the war. At the beginning of the war, Carey McWilliams expressed his unease with what he considered to be a spatially dense Japanese American population,

> ... when a large group of enemy aliens are concentrated in one area and when they are as easily recognizable as the Japanese, their position becomes almost intolerable ... theoretically, it enhances the possible menace of the group itself.[56]

The Myer–McWilliams' correspondence and the men's publications speak to their synergy.

In May 1943, Myer wrote to McWilliams expressing his appreciation of McWilliams' book, *Brothers Under the Skin*, in which McWilliams argues that, instead of a "Negro problem" or a "Japanese problem," there was a "race problem" caused by systemic racism. Although he did not acknowledge McWilliams' point about systemic racism, Myer wrote that he found the book's sections on "oriental minority racial problems" helpful. He expressed his belief in the importance of McWilliams' work: "It is the type of book every American should read."[57] In October 1944, Myer wrote to McWilliams praising McWilliams' latest book, *Prejudice; Japanese-Americans: Symbol of Racial Intolerance*, as a "masterpiece" and promised to do everything in his power to ensure a wide readership.[58] McWilliams wrote *Prejudice* with Myer's cooperation as WRA staff provided him information and he visited the Topaz, Utah, camp as part of his research.[59]

After the war, McWilliams applauded the WRA. Inconsistent in his criticism of the forced removal, he wrote:

> The evacuation has permanently changed the base of Japanese-American life in the United States. Thousands of the younger, better adjusted, more energetic [second generation Japanese Americans] are today permanently resettled outside of the West Coast and have no intention of returning. To some extent, this has been a favorable by-product of the evacuation program.

McWilliams continues: ". . . great credit is due the War Relocation Authority and its Director, Dillon S. Myer, for the excellent job that this agency did with an impossible assignment."[60]

Similarly positioned as white and university-educated, McWilliams, Myer, Tugwell, and the community analysts, who were overwhelmingly male, benefitted from the professional opportunities of white domination regardless that they depicted their professional roles as gender, race, and class-neutral. John Provinse took his experience from the BIA and the Soil Conservation Service to work as the WRA's Chief of Community Services. Scholars earned WRA salaries while advancing their careers. A 1940s list of Opler's publications includes those based on his studies of Japanese Americans and Native Americans. In correspondence about his publication in Columbia University's *Journal of American Folklore*, Opler comments, "we have no issues [of the journal] on this 'campus.'" With "campus," he was referring to a WRA camp. Rachel Sady worked as a community analyst while researching her thesis, "The Function and Control of Rumor in War Relocation Centers." The community analysts' supervisor, Edward Spicer, was on her thesis committee. In the Poston, Arizona, camp, where Navy Lieutenant Commander Leighton worked, researchers were able to earn University of Chicago credits through a program which also fast-tracked them to become Navy officers in the planned postwar occupation of Japan.[61]

Scholars cum civil servants applied social science theories. Although these concepts are not named in WRA documents, sociological terms such as "narrative of generations" and "race relations cycle" reverberated strongly throughout the WRA policy. Yu explains the Chicago scholars' narrative of generations theory, "the first generation tended to be insular and organize around 'traditional' Japanese or Chinese community norms, and the second generation tended to suffer from alienation from both 'oriental' and American communities."[62] Community analysts observed Japanese Americans using the word "Issei" for Japanese immigrants, "Nisei" for U.S.-born and raised Japanese Americans, and "Kibei" for those who were U.S.-born and raised, at least partly, in Japan. Observing this Japanese American vocabulary reinforced the WRA's emphasis on generations.[63] Indefinite leave codified the narrative of generations making it, at first, illegal, and later, extremely difficult for immigrants to gain even the semblance of freedom which came with indefinite leave.

Even though the narrative of generations paradigm was fundamental to WRA epistemology, not all WRA staff accepted it. Community analyst Rademaker departed from the narrative criticizing McWilliams and others who dismissed immigrants. Rademaker stayed within the assimilation framework, but other scholars' and policymakers' inability to see the extent of immigrants' adoption of Euro-American culture aggravated him. He believed that the WRA should have allowed immigrants more participation in Japanese Americans' social and geographical transformation.[64]

Myer and other administrators usually did not take community analysts' advice when it contradicted their policy goals. For example, McVoy felt that indefinite leave, which he called "dispersed integration," was impractical given Japanese Americans' culture and advocated for group leave to counter resistance to indefinite leave. He knew that leaving in groups would appeal more to Japanese Americans than doing so as individuals or as nuclear families and that his ideas were controversial. McVoy wrote, ". . . the WRA has been much opposed to the prospect of farming more Little Tokyos such that it probably will not reverse its position with regard to group resettlement to more than a limited extent."[65] He was right.

In May 1943, a WRA staff member reported to McVoy that some Japanese Americans were resisting indefinite leave and writing to people in other camps advising them to not leave unless the WRA offered more support. Having observed Japanese Americans' anger, McVoy repeatedly suggested that those who had been farmers be released to farm and be given financial support. The WRA did not prioritize group and farm leave over individual and urban leave, because the policy was to keep Japanese Americans as isolated from each other as possible.[66] The leave policy reflected Park's connection of "space" and "race." As Yu describes, "taking small isolated groups of Japanese. . . and spreading them across the American landscape, fit perfectly into the assimilation cycle's [also referred to as race relations cycle] definition of how to expose Orientals to American society."[67]

Before World War II, 90% of Japanese Americans on the continental United States lived on the West Coast. Although Japanese American geography recovered considerably, the forced removal, dispersion, and the lack of support for those who wanted to move back to the West Coast marked Japanese American demographics for decades. By the middle of 1947, only 55% of continental Japanese Americans lived on the West Coast. By 1950, the number was 60%, and by 1960, it was 70%. The highest percentage of Japanese Americans living on the West Coast since World War II was in 2000 when the number was 80%. As of 2015, six of the ten U.S. metropolitan areas with the largest Japanese populations were on the West Coast. They were Seattle and five California cities.[68]

Legacy

On Sunday, December 17, 1944, the War Department rescinded the exclusion orders effective on January 2, 1945. Deliberately, the rescission came after FDR's November 1944 reelection and before the U.S. Supreme Court's *Endo* decision. On December 18, 1944, the Court announced its unanimous decision that the WRA must free Endo, terminate the indefinite leave policy, and cease forcing "loyal" Japanese Americans to petition for release.[69]

The decision was not a victory for "the American way." Legal scholar Jerry Kang writes, "Endo technically released no one else."[70] He explains:

> . . . the Court expressly declined to address any of the constitutional issues. . . The "fall guy" was the War Relocation Authority (WRA) which, according to the Court, was never granted the power to detain concededly loyal American citizens such as Endo. . . Neither Endo nor, by proxy, the over 100,000 Japanese Americans interned, received public vindication that their *constitutional* rights had been violated. . .[71]

Instead of upholding the Constitution, in the majority opinion, the U.S. Supreme Court justices validated the WRA's indefinite leave policy as an assimilation program even as they ordered the program's termination. At the time, two-thirds of those originally imprisoned were still incarcerated. About this group, in 1971, Myer wrote, "probably half of them had never had it so good."[72]

The U.S. government terminated the WRA on June 30, 1946. Earlier that year, civil libertarian Alan Barth published a *Washington Post* editorial about the WRA titled, "Job Well Done," and that same year, several hundred Japanese American Citizens League members gathered in New York to honor Myer and thank him for his work. President Truman awarded Myer the Medal of Merit.[73]

Myer benefited from Presidential appointments and high-level international work until he retired in 1964 at the age of 73. He enjoyed prominent international affairs posts: Institute of Inter-American Affairs president, head of the United Nation's mission to the Middle East, senior expert in public administration for the United Nations in Venezuela. For short periods, he also worked for the U.S. Cuban refugee program, in the private sector, at the Agency for International Development, and with the Organization of American States. In 1946, Myer turned down the opportunity to become Puerto Rico's last nonelected governor stating that he did not want to spend time on diplomatic protocol and entertaining. Instead, he headed the Federal Public Housing Authority. Myer accepted the Bureau of Indian Affairs directorship in 1950 but had to resign in 1953 when a Republican president, Dwight Eisenhower, took over the White House.[74]

In 1971, Myer published *Uprooted Americans*, which incorporates his revisionist version of WRA history. This revision exemplifies what Lipsitz terms a "historical denial" and an "affirmation of white innocence."[75] Myer insists that the WRA greatly benefited those in its custody and that Japanese Americans were incarcerated due to their own choice, ". . . relocation centers. . . were way-stations for persons willing to resettle . . . or . . . temporary homes for those persons who wished to remain until they could return to their homes."[76] He also credits the WRA with a role in civil rights: "I feel the experience, actions, and results of the evacuation and relocation program has [sic] something to contribute to the civil rights programs of today."[77] He describes indefinite leave as the most important outcome of the "unnecessary evacuation" and maintains that the policy and his propaganda campaign facilitated the end of discriminatory laws, the growth of the Japanese American middle class, and the "cooperation of all folk of good will."[78]

Myer's revision of WRA history was also a revision of his own history. Like his depiction of his World War I civilian job, describing the "evacuation" as "unnecessary" is a "structuring contradiction" with which Myer utilizes a vulnerability to strengthen his overall depiction of himself as heroic.[79] Maintaining a public face in accordance with his masculinity ideology, he makes a nod to the injustice of the forced removal as he applauds himself for indefinite leave's "scattering."

While Myer was writing *Uprooted Americans*, young Japanese Americans were beginning to question their families' World War II experiences and connect the WRA to other manifestations of racism. He may well have been aware that he and the WRA would come under public scrutiny. In any case, Myer did not take responsibility for his leadership role in what Kang terms "the civil rights issue of the century."[80]

Robinson writes that, after World War II, the federal government "quickly changed from . . . violating the mass civil rights of Japanese-Americans to defending them before the Supreme Court against discriminatory California laws."[81] He does not, though, attribute this change to the WRA or Myer. Rather, Robinson sees it as a result of Japanese Americans' civil rights efforts and, particularly, of their contribution to the success of *Brown v. Board of Education*. In the *Stanford*

Law Review, Mary Dudziak connects *Brown*'s success, not to Myer or the WRA but, to U.S. government actors responsible for projecting an image of the United States as politically and culturally superior to the USSR.[82]

Along with the ideology of masculinity and wider cultural backgrounds described in Chapter 3, exploring the intersection between biography and history reveals that city and regional planning ideas and practices shaped Myer and the WRA. Indefinite leave is part of the planning legacy of social reformers for whom Americanness was something to bestow upon immigrants and their children. Reformers considered improving people's environments a method for improving the people themselves, and they applied it as an assimilation strategy. Like the social reform planning enacted upon earlier immigrants and their children, indefinite leave did not distinguish between reform and control. The policy also reflected the New Deal precedent of applying social science to improve the nation and target racially subordinated groups. Like the early social reformers, Myer and other New Dealers wanted to control the political and social behavior of immigrants and their children. He felt that their culture lacked a healthy dose of "American virtues."

In describing race and assimilation, Paul Kramer writes:

> . . . the relations of power between [two distinct, contracting parties] were defined not by the hegemon's outright exclusion of the less powerful but by its ability to establish and adjust standards or criteria for inclusion. In this way, the politics of recognition . . . required the subordinates to acknowledge, learn, and demonstrate their "assimilation" of the standards and the granting or withholding of power. Indeed, the subordinate party's acknowledged "success" in achieving these criteria affirmed and strengthened the hegemon's evaluative power.[83]

The WRA established and adjusted "standards for inclusion" for Japanese Americans. Those who wanted to leave the camps were required to strengthen white Americans' evaluative power by passing the loyalty exam, applying for indefinite leave, and obtaining WRA staff approval of their applications.

Indefinite leave illustrates the flexibility of cultural domination as Myer and other "white men in positions of influence and power" contributed to white hegemony and to the myth of white cultural superiority even while defending their policies to conservatives.[84] Conservatives rejected Japanese Americans as undeserving of admission into the U.S. body politic and of protection from mass violations while the liberal politics of recognition was also a politics of rejection. Liberals sought to expand U.S. national identity to include Japanese Americans but not their Japanese heritage. Myer did not let go of his belief in the superiority of Americanness over Japaneseness, English language over Japanese, and Christianity over Buddhism.

The U.S. government's World War II policies sent the message to Japanese Americans that military leaders, politicians, high-level officials, intelligentsia, and U.S. Supreme Court justices, "white men in positions of influence and power," found Japanese Americans' differences from the white middle-class suspect to the extent that the forced removal, incarceration, and indefinite leave were within the dominant understanding of sound policy.[85] The emotional impact of these violations are impossible to quantify. Filmmaker Renee Tajima-Pena shares that her mother "'believed the being too Japanese got her sent to the camps'" and, therefore, raised Tajima-Pena and her brother in Chicago to "just blend in."[86]

During World War II, Myer situated his defense of the WRA on American democratic ideals. In a January 1944 speech, he proclaimed,

> The WRA's work was in harmony with the best principles of our democratic past . . . the principle . . . which has guided our actions and molded our thinking is the belief that there is a place in this melting pot nation of ours for all people of goodwill and democratic faith who are now within our borders regardless of their racial antecedents.[87]

Decades later, Japanese American politicians, lawyers, and activists led a campaign to hold the United States accountable to its "best principles." These efforts included three *coram nobis* cases originally tried before the U.S. Supreme Court during World War II. In 1980, the U.S. Congress established an investigative commission, which determined that "racial prejudice, wartime hysteria, and a failure of political leadership" drove the forced removal and incarceration.[88]

Six years after Myer's death, Congress passed the Civil Liberties Act of 1988, and President Ronald Reagan signed it into law. Like *Brown*, the Act was a domestic milestone and partly catalyzed by U.S. foreign policy and international human rights discourse. Legal scholars, Yamamoto, Serrano, and Rodriguez, write that Reagan "shifted positions on reparations to bolster his administration's moral authority on human rights as the United States intensified the end stages of its war against world communism."[89]

The Civil Liberties Act of 1988 authorized $1.2 billion in reparations including $20,000 for each surviving Japanese American, the establishment of a public educational fund, and the issuance of a formal apology. The public education fund supported numerous academic, educational, and artistic endeavors including the research which provided the foundation for this book. President George H. Bush delivered the apology, which, along with reparations, was critical to the healing process of the surviving Japanese Americans and their descendants.[90]

Yamamoto refers to the reparations' legacy as "unfinished business" in his argument that Japanese Americans "must support the civil and human rights of others, or forfeit part of the moral foundation of Japanese American reparations."[91] The reparations have far-reaching significance as, in the United States and internationally, they are regularly cited as an example of a government's restitution for human rights violations. In the aftermath of the initial post-9/11 scapegoating and in response President Trump's policies, there is evidence of Japanese American solidarity with other "communities under siege."[92]

In 1941, President Roosevelt declared, "This nation has placed its destiny in the hands and heads and hearts of its free men and women. Freedom means the supremacy of *human rights* everywhere."[93] Roosevelt's statement was a criticism of Nazi Germany and a concealment of American realities. As President Donald Trump would during the so-called war on terror, FDR also used executive orders to direct human rights violations.[94]

Before and during World War II, a dominant idea among U.S. policymakers was that California was the home to an excessive number of Japanese Americans who posed a national security risk. From 2015 to the time of writing, German and American politicians on the right have claimed that uncontrollable amounts of refugees are overrunning their nations. Many believe that there is a "European migrant crisis" despite that 80–90 percent of refugees stay in their home regions and cannot afford to flee to Europe or North America. The United States is not among the countries that host the highest numbers of refugees and, of those on that list, only Turkey is in Europe.[95] This crisis in refugee politics and the controversies surrounding them and the U.S. and German heads of state, President Donald Trump and Chancellor Angela Merkel, serve as twenty-first-century examples of ideologies of white cultural superiority and gender. They are the subjects of Chapter 5.

Notes

1 Neil Genzlinger, "Time Marches... Backward!" *New York Times*, Sept. 2, 2010, www.nytimes.com/2010/09/03/movies/03newsreel.html. The "March of Time" series covered controversial topics and brought them to the forefront of public discourse.

2 Brian Hayashi, *Democratizing the Enemy* (Princeton, NJ: Princeton University Press, 2004), 180. Orin Starn, "Engineering Internment: Anthropologists and the War Relocation Authority," *American Ethnologist* 13, no. 4 (1986): 709.

3 Peter Irons, *Justice at War: The Story of the Japanese Internment Cases* (Berkeley, CA: University of California Press, 1983), 14.

4 *Ex parte Endo v. United States* (1944), 323 U.S. 283; 65 S. Ct. 208 at 211. Irons, 102–103.

5 Greg Robinson, *By Order of the President: FDR and the Internment of Japanese Americans* (Cambridge, MA: Harvard University Press, 2001), 180–181.

6 Warwick Anderson, *Colonial Pathologies: American Tropical Medicine, Race, and Hygiene in the Philippines* (Durham, NC: Duke University Press, 2006), 8.

7 The WRA bureaucrats and social scientists did not grasp that Japanese Americans were part of a multicultural society. They operated within a white Japanese paradigm.

8 Warwick Anderson, 8. Ronald Takaki, *A Different Mirror: A History of Multicultural America* (New York: Little, Brown and Co., 2008), 135, 262–291.

9 Maurice Broady, *Planning for People: Essays on the Social Context of Planning* (London: National Council of Social Service, 1968).

10 Richard Fogelsong, *Planning the Capitalist City: The Colonial Era to the 1920s* (Princeton, NJ: Princeton University Press, 1986), 67–68.

11 Barbara Hooper, "'Split at the Roots': A Critique of the Philosophical and Political Sources of Modern Planning Doctrine," *Frontiers*, 13, no. 1, (1992): 45–79. Anthony E. Rotundo, *American Manhood: Transformations in Masculinity from the Revolution to the Modern Era* (New York: Basic Books, 1993), 220. Mel Scott, *American City Planning since 1890* (Berkeley, CA: University of California Press, 1971), 368–471.

12 Thomas S. Hines, *Burnham of Chicago: Architect and Planner* (Chicago, IL: University of Chicago, 1974).

13 John Friedmann, *Planning in the Public Domain: From Knowledge to Action* (Princeton, NJ: Princeton University Press, 1987), 106–112. J.Y. Smith, "Rexford Tugwell, Adviser in FDR's 'Brains Trust,' Dies," *Washington Post*, July 25, 1979, www.washingtonpost.com/archive/local/1979/07/25/rexford-tugwell-adviser-in-fdrs-brains-trust-dies/68a9b1c6-d8c3-44f7-b7d0-2599bada50c4/?noredirect=on&utm_term=.fd423246b388.

14 Friedmann, 106–112. J.Y. Smith, "Rexford Tugwell." Rexford G. Tugwell, *The Place of Planning in Society: Seven Lectures on the Place of Planning in Society with Special Reference to Puerto Rico* (San Juan: Puerto Rico Planning Board, 1954), 43, 78, 79, 81.

15 J.Y. Smith, "Rexford Tugwell." Richard Drinnon, *Keeper of Concentration Camps: Dillon S. Myer and American Racism* (Berkeley, CA: University of California Press, 1987), 44.

16 Tugwell, *The Place*, 76. Tugwell's conception of the world was peculiarly male as was that of the vast majority of social scientists of his generation.

17 Paul A. Kramer, *The Blood of Government: Race Empire, the United States, and the Philippines* (Chapel Hill, NC: University of North Carolina Press, 2006). James Walvin, "Symbols of Moral Superiority: Slavery, Sport and the Changing World Order, 1800–1950," in *Manliness and Morality: Middle-Class Masculinity in Britain and America, 1800–1940*, eds. J.A. Mangan and James Walvin (Manchester: Manchester University Press, 1987), 252. Kramer uses "the blood of government" to refer to the belief in an innate ability to lead.

18 Anderson, 159.

19 Dillon S. Myer, *Uprooted Americans: The Japanese Americans and the War Relocation Authority during World War II* (Tucson, AZ: University of Arizona Press, 1971), 6. Starn, 715–716.

20 Harvey Sitkoff, *A New Deal for Blacks: The Emergence of Civil Rights as a National Issue* (New York: Oxford University Press, 1978), 43–47, 48, 52–55.

21 Ibid, 48.

22 Ibid, 67, 68. Tony Badger, "New Deal," in *Encyclopedia of the Great Depression*, ed. Robert S. McElvaine, Vol. 2 (New York: Macmillan Reference USA, 2004), 701–711, *Gale Virtual Reference Library*, http://link.galegroup.com/apps/doc/CX3404500395/GVRL?u=csus_main&sid=GVRL&xid=61d8392b.

23 Sitkoff, 59, 67–68, 72, 82. From 1922 to 1941, Italy imposed apartheid on Eritrea, which it had dominated since 1889, and Eritrea's capital, Asmara, became the capital of Italian East Africa. Mussolini sought to recover the power of the Holy Roman Empire and used Eritrea as a launching ground for his 1935 invasion of Ethiopia.

24 Michael Hibbard, "Public Epistemologies and Policy Planning: The Case of American Indian Policy" (Ph.D. diss., University of California Los Angeles, 1980), 158.

25 Ibid., 134, 158, 161, 162. While many Native Americans welcomed Collier's administrative paradigm shift, perspectives on the IRA varied strongly among Native Nations. Regardless of Native opinion, in 1934, the IRA ended allotment, which had been federal policy since the 1887 Dawes Act. Allotment broke up communal land into individual parcels, which the federal government held in trust. From 1887 to 1934, two-thirds of land formerly owned by Native Americans had become non-Natives' property.

26 Lawrence Kelly, "Anthropology in the Soil Conservation Service," *Agricultural History* 59, no. 2 (1985): 135–147.

27 Ibid., 135–147. See Paul A. Kramer, "The Pragmatic Empire: U.S. Anthropology and Colonial Politics in the Occupied Philippines, 1896–1916" (Ph.D. diss., Princeton University, 1998), and Paul A. Kramer, "Making Concessions: Race and Empire Revisited at the Philippine Exposition, St. Louis, 1901–05," *Radical History Review*, 73 (1999): 74–114. Kelly, 140–143.

28 Ibid. Edward B. Marks, Jr., to John H. Provinse, Oct. 8, 1943, WRA Papers Headquarters-Subject-Classified General Files, File 2 Jan to Dec 1943, 71.100, RG 210, National Archives Building, Washington, D.C. Ottis Peterson to William H. Tolbert, Nov. 23, 1945, RG 210, Washington Office Records Chronological File-General-Alph Folder Agriculture Dept. of Dec 1942–Aug 1945, 71.100, RG 210, National Archives Building, Washington,

D.C. Ottis Peterson to Adon Poli, Sept. 5, 1945, Washington Office Records Chronological File-General-Alph Folder Agriculture Dept. of Dec 1942–Aug 1945, 71.100, RG 210, National Archives Building, Washington, D.C. Dillon S. Myer, *An Autobiography of Dillon S. Myer* (Berkeley, CA: University of California, 1970), 253. The closeness between the WRA and the Department of Agriculture continued throughout the WRA's existence with the agencies sharing information and staff including Japanese Americans even after the war was over. A letter from the WRA Relocation Division Acting Chief to a USDA staff member pertains to Japanese Americans who worked for the Department of Agriculture in Oregon. The Department of Agriculture staff requested information on Japanese Americans' movements and asked to be added to the WRA's mailing list. When Myer took over the BIA, Provinse was already there as an Assistant Commissioner. Provinse wrote his dissertation on indigenous social control methods. Provinse and Kimball did not get the chance to realize their plan as the SCS terminated the experiment before its completion. Kimball insisted that the plan would have resulted in implementing policies without coercion.

29 Carey McWilliams, *Brothers under the Skin* (Boston, MA: Little, Brown & Co., 1964), 50–78. "California and the Japanese," Feb. 10, 1942, Carey McWilliams Collection, Special Collections, Young Research Library, UCLA, Los Angeles. Roger Daniels, *The Decision to Relocate the Japanese Americans* (Philadelphia, PA: Lippincott, 1975), 6, 31, 50, 36–39. Carey McWilliams, *Factories in the Field: The Story of Migratory Farm Labor in California* (Berkeley, CA: University of California Press, 1999).

30 "Town Meeting," "Aspects of Post-War Planning," "Migration and Resettlement of the People," Personal Memorandum, Carey McWilliams Collection, Special Collections, Young Research Library, UCLA, Los Angeles. McWilliams, *Brothers*, 77. Kelly, 146, 147. Reflecting the web of networks shared by these scholars and public officials, McWilliams thanked Eshrev Shevky in his acknowledgements in *Brothers under the Skin*.

31 Sitkoff, 48, 61–65, 195. Warwick Anderson, 10.

32 Sitkoff, 198.

33 Ibid, 194. McWilliams, *Brothers*, 15, 79.

34 Alexander H. Leighton, *The Governing of Men: General Principles and Recommendations Based on Experience at a Japanese Relocation Camp* (Princeton, NJ: Princeton University Press, 1945), appendix. He co-authored, "Applied Anthropology in a Dislocated Community," with Edward Spicer who supervised WRA community analysts.

35 Starn, 716.

36 Ibid., 706. Marvin Opler to John Embree, June 25, 1943, M.E. and M.K. Opler, Records of the United States War Relocation Authority, MS 42, Special Collections, University of Arizona Library, Tucson.

37 John Rademaker to John Embree, July 23, 1943, John Rademaker, Records of the United States War Relocation Authority, MS 42, Special Collections, University of Arizona Library, Tucson. Edward Spicer to John Embree, June 25, 1943, John Embree, Records of the War Relocation Authority, MS 42, Special Collections, University of Arizona Library, Tucson.

38 Dillon S. Myer, Director, "Constitutional Principles involved in the Relocation Program," Presented Before the Costello Sub-committee of House Committee of Un-American Activities, June 6, 1943, WRA Headquarters,

WRA Paper Headquarters-Subject-Classified General, Jan. to Dec. 1943, 71.100, RG 210, National Archives Building, Washington, D.C.

39 Starn, 706.

40 Ibid.

41 Henry Yu, "Thinking about Orientals: Modernity, Social Science, and Asians in Twentieth-Century America" (Ph.D. diss., Princeton University, 1995), 57. John A. Rademaker to John Embree, July 23, 1943, John A. Rademaker, Records of the United States War Relocation Authority.

42 Henry Yu, *Thinking Orientals: Migration, Contact, and Exoticism in Modern America* (New York: Oxford University Press, 2001), 47.

43 Yu, "Thinking about Orientals," 335.

44 Maureen T. Hallinan, ed., *Handbook of the Sociology of Education* (New York: Springer, 2006).

45 Yu, "Thinking about Orientals," 180–181.

46 Marvin Opler to John Embree, June 25, 1943, Records of the United States War Relocation Authority, MS 42, Special Collections, University of Arizona Library, Tucson. Opler also mentions that Japanese Americans saw the community analysts as liaisons who may have been able to deliver complaints to the WRA. This raises the question as to whether the researchers were "in" with Japanese Americans or if Japanese Americans viewed the researchers as tools which they could utilize to improve their circumstances.

47 John Rademaker to John Embree, July 30, 1943, John Rademaker, MS 42, Special Collections, University of Arizona Library, Tucson. Leighton, 6. Starn, 706. Psychiatrist Alexander Leighton viewed acts of resistance like the Poston strike as "sudden diseases of society."

48 Different stances toward the WRA often caused tension among Japanese Americans. They seemed to assume that Japanese Americans did not know why they were angry.

49 Leighton, 373. Robert Redfield to Dillon S. Myer, Apr. 12, 1943, Personal Correspondence 1943, Myer Papers, Truman Library, Independence, MO. Dillon S. Myer to E.H. Bond, Jan. 25, 1945, Personal Correspondence 1945, Myer Papers, Truman Library, Independence, MO. By the end of World War II, Myer's oldest daughter was attending the University of Chicago.

50 Edgar McVoy to Edward Spicer, Apr. 28, 1943 and July 10, 1943, Edgar McVoy, Records of the United States War Relocation Authority, MS 42, Special Collections, University of Arizona Library, Tucson. McVoy wanted to get more Japanese Americans out of the camp as he knew it was a substandard environment. To this end, his family employed a Japanese American who had been incarcerated in Jerome as a domestic servant in their Washington, D.C. home. In so doing, McVoy was following Secretary of the Interior Harold Ickes' example. Ickes employed Japanese Americans as farm hands. McVoy also arranged for his oldest child's well-being by moving his family out of the camp where they had been living with him and made sure that his wife gave birth to their second child in Washington, D.C. even though that meant that he would be separated from her.

51 WRA Headquarters, June 6, 1943, WRA Paper Headquarters-Subject-Classified General, Jan. to Dec. 1943, 71.100, RG 210, National Archives Building, Washington, D.C.

52 "Ansel Adams's Photographs of Japanese-American Internment at Manzanar – Background and Scope," Library of Congress, accessed Oct. 18, 2018, www.loc.gov/pictures/collection/manz/. Adams' and Miyatake's photographs are visual euphemisms which mask the fact that Japanese Americans were incarcerated. This was an intentional strategy to downplay that they were incarcerated as their incarceration validated yellow peril fears in many white Americans minds. Dorothea Lange's photographs are "bleak."

53 Elena Tajima Creef, *Imaging Japanese America: The Visual Construction of Citizenship, Nation, and the Body* (New York: New York University Press, 2004), 9, 18, 21. See also Ansel Adams, *Born Free and Equal: Photographs of Loyal Japanese-Americans in Manzanar Relocation Center, Inyo, California* (New York: U.S. Camera, 1944).

54 See Margaret R. Higonnet, Jane Jenson, Sonya Michel, and Margaret Collins Weitz, *Behind the Lines: Gender and the Two World Wars* (New Haven, CT: Yale University Press, 1987), 23. Usually, governments use propaganda to change people's perceptions and use fear-mongering to mobilize them to support a war or encourage them to take on new roles. In this case, the government used propaganda to assuage people's fears and convince them to view Japanese Americans as comforting and familiar instead of frightening and alien.

55 United States War Relocation Authority, *The Relocation Program* (Washington, D.C.: U.S. Government Printing Office, 1946).

56 "California and the Japanese," Feb. 10, 1942, Carey McWilliams Collection, Special Collections, Young Research Library, UCLA, Los Angeles. Drinnon, 94.

57 Dillon S. Myer to Carey McWilliams, May 15, 1943, 71.100, RG 210, Washington Office Records Chronological File General–Alphabetical Folder MCL-MCZ, National Archives Building, Washington, D.C.

58 Carey McWilliams, *Prejudice; Japanese Americans: A Symbol of Racial Intolerance* (Boston, MA: Little, Brown & Co., 1944).

59 Dillon S. Myer to Carey McWilliams, Oct. 24, 1944 and June 24, 1943, and Carey McWilliams to Dillon S. Myer, May 21, 1943, Washington Office Records Chronological File General–Alphabetical Folder MCL-MCZ, 71.100, RG 210, National Archives Building, Washington, D.C. McWilliams offered his services to the WRA as a consultant. Myer, who was not interested in hiring consultants, offered McWilliams positions as Minidoka camp project attorney and assistant director of a California camp. McWilliams turned down both of these offers.

60 "The Meaning of Wartime Exile," Carey McWilliams Collection, Special Collections, Young Research Library, UCLA, Los Angeles.

61 Leighton, 373. Marvin Opler, n.d., M.E. and M.K. Opler, Records of the United States War Relocation Authority, MS 42, Special Collections, University of Arizona Library, Tucson. Edward Spicer to Rachel Sady Jan. 7, 1946, Rachel Sady, Records of the United States War Relocation Authority, MS 42, Special Collections, University of Arizona Library, Tucson. Hayashi, 24.

62 Yu, "Thinking about Orientals," 176–179.

63 Ibid., 177–179. Leighton, 70–80.

64 John A. Rademaker to Edward Spicer, Jan. 25, 1945, John A. Rademaker, Records of the United States War Relocation Authority, MS 42, Special Collections, University of Arizona Library, Tucson.

65 Edgar McVoy to John Embree, Aug. 2, 1943, Edgar McVoy, Records of the United States War Relocation Authority, MS 42, Special Collections, University of Arizona Library, Tucson. Leland Barrow, Acting Director, WRA to all project directors, Oct. 28, 1943, WRA Papers Headquarters-Subject-Classified Gen. Files, File 2 Jan. to Dec. 1943, 71.100, RG 210, National Archives Building, Washington, D.C. Although the idea did become, at least briefly, a topic of official discussion, the WRA did not reverse its position on group resettlement.

66 Edgar McVoy to John Embree, May 6, 1943, Records of the United States War Relocation Authority, MS 42, Special Collections, University of Arizona Library, Tucson. Michiko Tanaka and Akemi Kikumura-Yano, *Through Harsh Winters: The Life of a Japanese Immigrant Woman* (Novato, CA: Chandler & Sharp, 1981). Tanaka chronicles her family's leaving a WRA camp to become tenant farmers.

67 Yu, *Thinking*, 188.

68 Roger Daniels, *Concentration Camps, USA: Japanese Americans and World War II* (New York: Holt, Rinehart and Winston, 1971), 166–167. "Top 10 U.S. Metropolitan Areas by Japanese Population, 2015," Japanese in the U.S. Fact Sheet, Pew Research Center's Social & Demographic Trends, Sept. 8, 2017, www.pewsocialtrends.org/fact-sheet/asian-americans-japanese-in-the-u-s/. From Roger Daniels numbers, it seems that, between 1950 and 1960, 10 percent of the continental Japanese American population moved back to California, Oregon, and Washington from the Midwest and East Coast where many had resettled. The other four cities with the largest Japanese American populations in 2015 were Honolulu, New York, Chicago, and Washington, D.C.

69 Dorothy Swaine Thomas with Charles Kikuchi and James Minoru Sakoda, *The Salvage* (Berkeley, CA: University of California Press, 1952), 113. Patrick O. Gudridge, "Remember Endo?" *Harvard Law Review* 116, no. 1933 (2003): 1935.

70 Jerry Kang, "Watching the Watchers: Enemy Combatants in the Internment's Shadow," *Law and Contemporary Problems* 68, no. 2 (2005): 261, https://scholarship.law.duke.edu/lcp/vol68/iss2/

71 Jerry Kang, "Denying Prejudice: Internment, Redress, and Denial," *UCLA Law Review* 51, (2004): 959, 960. Emphasis in the original.

72 Irons, 99–100. Myer, *Uprooted Americans*, 292.

73 Drinnon, 9.

74 Ibid., 9, 164–166, 249, 250.

75 George Lipsitz, *The Possessive Investment in Whiteness: How White People Profit from Identity Politics* (Philadelphia, PA: Temple University Press, 2018), 264, ProQuest Ebook Central, https://ebookcentral.proquest.com/lib/csus/detail.action?docID=5425334.

76 Myer, *Uprooted Americans*, xiv.

77 Ibid.

78 Ibid, xv, 286.

79 Stanley I. Thangaraj, *Desi Hoop Dreams: Pickup Basketball and the Making of Asian American Masculinity* (New York: New York University Press, 2015), 23.

80 Kang, "Denying," 964.

81 Greg Robinson, Jerry Kang, and Hiroshi Motomura, "A Symposium on Greg Robinson's A Tragedy of Democracy: Japanese Confinement

in North America," *Asian Pacific American Law Journal* 15, no. 1 (June 2010): 7.

82 Ibid., 8. Mary L. Dudziak, "Desegregation as a Cold War Imperative," *Stanford Law Review* 41, no. 1 (1988): 61–120, doi:10.2307/1228836, quoted in Eric K. Yamamoto, Susan K. Serrano and Michelle Natividad Rodriguez, "American Racial Justice on Trial—Again: African American Reparations, Human Rights, and the War on Terror," *Michigan Law Review* 101, no. 5 (Mar. 2003): 1269–1337, doi:10.2307/3595376.

83 Kramer, *The Blood*, 18.

84 Ronald Takaki, *Hiroshima: Why America Dropped the Atomic Bomb* (Boston, MA: Little, Brown, and Co., 1995), 8–9.

85 Takaki, *Hiroshima*, 8–9.

86 Creef, 3.

87 Dillon S. Myer, "The Facts of the War Relocation Authority," Jan. 21, 1944, WRA Speech, Myer Papers, Truman Library, Independence, MO.

88 *Korematsu v. United States*, 584 F. Supp. 1406 (N.D. Cal. 1984), *Hirabayashi v. United States*, 828 F.2d 591 (9th Cir. 1987) (vacating the conviction of Gordon Hirabayashi, which was originally affirmed in *Hirabayashi v. United States*, 320 U.S. 81 (1943), *Yasui v. United States*, 772 F.2d 1496 (9th Cir. 1985) reopening *Yasui v. United States*, 320 U.S. 115 (1943), cited in Yamamoto, Serrano, and Rodriguez, 1273–1277. Norman Y. Mineta, "I Was Detained in a U.S. Internment Camp. Here's Why America's Current Tragedies Have the Same Causes," *Time*, June 21, 2018, http://time.com/5318234/americas-recent-horrors-echo-its-history/.

89 Yamamoto, Serrano, and Rodriguez, 1276.

90 Library of Congress, "Ansel Adams's." Yamamoto, Serrano, and Rodriguez, 1269, 1276. Kang, "Denying," 976. Jerry Kang points out that the executive and legislative branches of the government participated in the apology and reparations, but "the Judiciary did not quite do what is commonly supposed. . . it cloaked itself in denial."

91 Erik K. Yamamoto, "Beyond Redress: Japanese Americans' Unfinished Business," *Asian Law Journal* 7 (Jan. 2000): 131, https://doi.org/10.15779/Z38KW15, quoted in Yamamoto, Serrano and Rodriguez, 1277. Yamamoto adds, "No one is suggesting that. . . Japanese Americans are doing this. But in theory the possibility remains."

92 Yamamoto, Serrano, and Rodriguez, 1269–1270. "JACL Submits Amicus Brief to SCOTUS in Opposition to Muslim Travel Ban," Japanese American Citizen League, accessed Dec. 30, 2018, https://jacl.org/jacl-submits-amicus-brief-to-scotus-in-opposition-to-muslim-travel-ban/. Kathy Masaoka, "'Communities under Siege: Keeping the Faith' Fourth Break the Fast Event," *Nikkei for Civil Rights and Redress*, Accessed Dec. 30, 2018, www.ncrr-la.org/news/2-8-05/2.html.

93 Ronald Takaki, *A Different Mirror: A History of Multicultural America* (New York: Back Bay Books, 2008), 341. Emphasis in the original.

94 "Executive Order Protecting the Nation from Foreign Terrorist Entry into the United States," Jan. 27, 2017, White House, www.whitehouse.gov/presidential-actions/executive-order-protecting-nation-foreign-terrorist-entry-united-states/. Takaki, *A Different Mirror*, 371–380.

95 See, for example, BBC News, "Migrant Crisis: EU Leaders Plan Secure Migrant Centres," June 29, 2018, www.bbc.com/news/world-europe-44652846. DW, "AfD." "Figures at a Glance," UNHCR. "California and the Japanese," Feb. 10, 1942, Carey McWilliams Collection, Special Collections, Young Research Library, UCLA, Los Angeles. Drinnon, 94. At the beginning of the war, Carey McWilliams expressed his unease with what he considered to be a spatially dense Japanese American population, ". . . when a large group of enemy aliens are concentrated in one area and when they are as easily recognizable as the Japanese, their position becomes almost intolerable . . . theoretically, it enhances the possible menace of the group itself."

5 Epilogue

Racism and nationalism in the twenty-first century

Photo 9 Chancellor Merkel and President Trump during the Second Day of the 2018 G7 Summit.

Source: Denzel, Jesco, photographer. *German Chancellor Angela Merkel and the American President Donald Trump during the second day of the G7 Summit in Charlevoix, Canada / photograph by Jesco Denzel.* 2018. Photograph. www.laif.de #20646280.

> We are celebrating the 230th anniversary of our beloved Constitution. . . The United States is a compassionate nation, and has spent billions and billions of dollars in helping to [provide for refugees] . . .
>
> —President Trump[1]

> What did the founding fathers of Europe mean when they said nationalism will lead to war again? . . . let's not start dividing ourselves into groups again.
>
> —Chancellor Merkel[2]

Since 2015, racist nationalism has increasingly endangered people seeking safe havens in the United States and Europe. While after September 11, 2001, the United States' vetting of refugees became more stringent, the most dramatic changes in U.S. refugee policy have been in 2017 and 2018—the Trump administration's first years. In part a reaction to the 2005 Madrid terrorist attack and those in France in 2015 and Germany in 2016, European policies have also become more restrictive, and Germany has seen particularly dramatic shifts.[3] U.S. President Donald Trump's administration, German Chancellor Angela Merkel's government, and the rhetoric and policies of their refugee crises serve as twenty-first-century examples of white cultural superiority and gender ideologies.

Globally, 2017 saw a record high number of 68.5 million people displaced by political violence including 28.5 million forced out of their countries. Despite the historic need for safe havens, in 2018, the United States and Germany will admit fewer refugees than they did in 2015. In 2015, Germany admitted 890,000 people, and 1.5 million were admitted by the fall of 2017. The United States set its 2018 refugee cap at 45,000, the lowest number since 1980, but is likely to admit less than 22,000 people. Mrs. Merkel as during World War II, policies which are supposedly about national security have been part of attacks on human rights including on the rights of people to flee harm. While the term "migrant" is frequently used in both countries, the word conceals the fact that many of these newcomers and would-be newcomers are seeking political asylum or refuge from war and are, therefore, entitled by U.S., German, and international laws to certain rights including the right to enter a country without passports or visas and apply for asylum.[4]

President Trump

As FDR did and many other U.S. presidents have, President Trump claims that the United States places a particularly high value on human rights. Human rights rhetoric is part of the narrative which he employs to portray the United States as superior to other nations and, especially, to non-Euro-American nations, yet his administration has been eroding human rights. He attempts to justify this erosion by depicting non-Europeans and non-Christians as culturally inferior to the United States' dominant Euro-American Christian majority and, therefore, as threatening to U.S. national identity and undeserving of protection.

In addition to being racist, Trump's refugee policies and policy rhetoric are gendered and patriarchal. In his speech announcing his candidacy for the Republican Presidential nomination, Trump claimed,

> When Mexico sends its people, they're not sending their best. They're not sending you. They're not sending you . . . They're bringing crime. They're rapists. . . from all over South and Latin America, and it's coming probably—probably—from the Middle East. . . Islamic terrorism is eating up large portions of the Middle East.[5]

Trump contrasted people from Lain America and the Middle East with the prospective voters in his audience, "They're not sending you." He and others on the U.S. right utilize gendered stereotypes labeling newcomers as "rapists," "criminals," and "terrorists."[6] Denying racist intent, they contend that their anti-refugee policies are motivated by concern for national security and the safety of Americans, especially women, from sexual assault and other violent crimes. The president claims to be "totally opposed to domestic violence," yet his administration has reduced support for survivors of domestic violence and sexual assault in domestic and refugee policies. Under Trump's administration, domestic violence has been eliminated as grounds for political asylum.[7]

Along with an agenda to erode women's rights, Trump places a high value on a certain type of toughness as did the Imperial and Bourgeois Brothers. Despite that he is not part of the Bourgeois Brothers' middle-class or the Imperials' elite class, he shares this significant aspect of his masculinity ideology with the Brotherhoods. Part of Trump's toughness stems from his resentment of the elite. While Trump was born into a wealthy family in Queens in New York City, from a young age, he was aware of the much wealthier and more powerful multigenerational elites of Manhattan.[8]

Like the Imperials, Trump attended a boys-only boarding school, which "imbue[d] men with a particular kind of 'manhood.'"[9] This manhood is homosocial and combative like the male-centered "high" level "struggles over political inclusion."[10] Even though he had two brothers, Donald was the only Trump child sent away. Trump was sent to boarding school, because his father was fed up with his poor behavior whereas boys born into elite families attended boarding school because of their class and family traditions.[11]

According to the PBS documentary, *The Choice, 2016*, Fred Trump sent Donald, "to the toughest boarding school he could find, the New York Military Academy. . . [which] was no-nonsense, heavy on discipline, [and] over the years home to the children of gangster John Gotti and Cuban dictator Fulgencio Batista."[12] The school had an intense culture of violent hazing to which all students were subjected, and doing gender, young Donald demonstrated his toughness in this violent environment by successfully competing in sports and garnering his peers' admiration as a "ladies man."[13] As it did for the Brothers, for Trump, doing gender includes behaviors, actions, and attitudes toward women, which were part of his socialization from an early age.

After graduating from the Wharton School of Finance and Commerce, Trump joined his father's business with the goal of succeeding in Manhattan real estate. He modeled his lifestyle after that of Hugh Hefner who symbolized a postsexual revolution masculinity. One commentator characterizes Trump's masculinity as that of a "hypermasculine New York hustler" and distinct from that of President Obama who, like Dwight Eisenhower, "emulated" George Washington's "stoic dignity."[14]

Dean reports that the Kennedy and Johnson administrations were obsessed with "'toughness' and the use of sexualized language of competition and dominance."[15] Trump publicly uses such language in his tweets and elsewhere whereas Truman, Kennedy, and Johnson, for example, used it behind closed doors. Trump's martial metaphors and masculinist rhetoric mark his international negotiations and domestic politics. For example, his exchanges with North Korean leader, Kim Jong Un, have the hallmarks of Truman's negotiations with Stalin replete with associating bombs with virility.[16]

On January 27, 2017, the month of his inauguration, Trump signed the "Executive Order Protecting the Nation from Foreign Terrorist Entry into the United States," which banned people from seven Muslim-majority countries from entering the United States for 90 days, halted refugee resettlement for 120 days, and banned Syrian refugees indefinitely. This policy, known as the "Muslim ban," signaled that the values and tactics of his campaign would extend into Trump's presidency.[17] Titled and promoted as a national security initiative, the president successfully strategized for the order to give him the advantage of surprise over his adversaries.[18]

During Trump's campaign and first seven months in the White House, Steve Bannon served as his Chief Strategist. According to *The New York Times*' Peter Baker, the ban was, "[Steve] Bannon's idea . . . to . . . knock [everyone] back before they have a chance to resist."[19] Journalist Robert Costa reports, "Trump has told me multiple times that he actually loves to fight. In Bannon, he saw someone who was just like him, someone who loved to fight."[20]

The order alienated millions of people within and outside of the United States and put American human rights groups on the defensive. In June 2018, the U.S. Supreme Court ruled to reverse lower courts' decisions that the ban was unconstitutional. As with the World War II Japanese American U.S. Supreme Court cases, a future generation of justices may very well decide to issue a writ of *coram nobis* to correct this fundamental error.[21]

While the Muslim ban was in the lower courts, Trump addressed the United Nations where he invoked the U.S. Constitution as a symbol of advanced political culture and global leadership. Citing U.S. refugee policy as an example of the nation's leadership in human rights, he contrasted the United States to other countries whose inclusion in the U.N. Human Rights Council Trump described as a "massive source of embarrassment to the United Nations." Again, depicting the United States as if it is on a higher plane, he stated, "The American people hope that one day soon the United Nations can be a much more accountable and effective advocate for human dignity and freedom around the world. . ."[22]

The U.N. Office of the High Commissioner on Human Rights had accused nine Council member countries of retaliating against their citizens for cooperating with U.N. human rights investigations. Nonetheless, Trump's portrayal of the United States, its refugee policy, and Americans as especially enlightened about human rights is at odds with U.S. history and Trump's own policies. As an American Civil Liberties Union human rights expert stated, the president "undermine[s] human rights and international bodies."[23] In 2018, *The Washington Post* reported that Trump "downplayed" other countries' human rights abuses when he thought it served him to do so.[24] Also, in 2018, Trump's national security advisor threatened to sanction the International Criminal Court and its judges and prosecutors if they approved an investigation of U.S. torture in Afghanistan, and Trump refused to appear at a hearing of the Inter-American Commission on Human Rights.[25]

Trump's child separation policy further reflects a disregard for human rights and the combative toughness, which is still part of doing gender in Washington. Starting in April 2018, Trump and Attorney General Jeff Sessions chose to prosecute all adults who entered the United States without legal documents including those who wanted to apply for asylum. *The Washington Post* reports that

> Undocumented immigrant families seeking asylum previously were released and went into the civil court system, but [in 2018] the parents [were] detained and sent to criminal courts while their kids [were] resettled in the United States as though they were unaccompanied minors.[26]

In the midst of the child separation controversy, Trump tweeted, "Big mistake made all over Europe in allowing millions of people in who have so strongly and violently changed their culture!" and claimed, "crime in Germany is way up."[27] Official figures contradicted Trump as German crime was at its lowest since 1992.[28] The president's contention that "millions" had "violently" changed European "culture" was an invitation for Americans to find parallels between the United States and Germany and view the victims of the child separation policy as threats to Americans' safety and culture.

Trump's intention was to use the child separation policy as political leverage in Congressional negotiations prompting him to publicly attribute it to the Democrats and falsely claim that an executive order could not overturn it. His plans, though, were thwarted as the policy proved controversial even within his own political party. On June 20, 2018, Trump signed an executive order ending the policy. While the Trump administration was responsible for child separation, Trump's attempt to employ it to negotiate with Congress says as much about Washington, D.C.'s political culture as it does about this individual president. As with military masculinity, in Washington politics, people of all genders find it advantageous to cultivate tough images.[29]

Like the Cold War leaders who kept the United States in a losing war in South East Asia, Trump associates loss with vulnerability and resoluteness with strength. Dillon Myer claimed to have no regrets about his role in Japanese Americans' human rights violations. Truman hid regret about the atomic bombings behind a public mask of resolve. Similarly, after ending child separation, Trump maintained his antirefugee stance.

Trump's ambassador to the U.N., Nikki Haley, disagreed with him on some refugee policies, because she believed that they were detrimental to United States' allies. Nonetheless, she defended many of his policies including those which impacted human rights such as the United States' withdrawal from negotiations over the Global Compact on Migration and the administration's attack on a U.N. human rights investigation of U.S. poverty. Although Trump "chaffed at her ambition," according to *The Washington Post*, Haley was one of the most influential people in his administration and was even more influential than the Secretary of State.[30] In addition to her work at the UN, as a woman, Haley has another quality that the president values. Journalist Bob Woodward reports that, like Hope Hicks, the President's campaign press secretary, Haley has "the glamourous look Trump liked."[31]

Haley's October 2018 resignation provides a significant glimpse into gender in the Trump White House. During the announcement of her resignation, Haley, a 46 year-old and a former governor of South Carolina, created a verbal diminution by referring to herself as a "girl," "I'm such a lucky girl to have been able to lead the state that raised me and to serve a country I love so very much has really been a blessing, and I want to thank you for that," she told Trump. Trump said that the ambassadorship had become "more glamorous" during the time it was held by Haley.[32]

Gender and masculinity ideologies, the idea of white cultural superiority and a Euro-American, Christian-dominated national identity shape U.S. refugee policy formation, implementation, and rhetoric including the interactions between the president and senior members of his administration. Trump's policies demonstrate his operationalization of, what Henry Giroux calls, "an imagined community organized around the symbols of fear and disposability in which the nation is deemed synonymous with a white Christian public sphere."[33] With claims of national security concerns and depictions of newcomers as threats, within its first two years, the Trump administration has dramatically reduced the numbers of refugees admitted to the United States and changed the demographics of U.S. refugees. The proportion of Muslims among refugees allowed into the United States has decreased and the proportion of Europeans has increased despite that the two biggest refugee-producing conflicts in the world are in Syria and Yemen—middle eastern, Muslim-majority countries.[34]

Chancellor Merkel

In the tweet claiming that refugees had "strongly and violently changed [European] culture," Trump also declared, "The people of Germany are turning against their leadership. . ."[35] While this language is misleading considering that Chancellor Merkel and her party were still in power, there is some truth to the claim. The number of people claiming asylum in Germany has fallen each year since 2015, yet the issue is, arguably, Germany's most controversial political topic and the main reason for the chancellor's political decline.[36] The debates surrounding Chancellor Merkel and German refugee policy demonstrate the enduring strength of the idea of white cultural superiority and of gender ideology.

As in the United States, in Germany, the controversies surrounding refugee policies are at the heart of the identity of an increasingly divided nation. The divisions manifest in demonstrations, counterdemonstrations, and at the polls. Merkel's power has decreased as that of white nationalists and the Green Party has increased. While, as Lipsitz observers,

Trump enjoyed the "Overwhelming support from white voters . . . [and] secure[d] the presidency, largely by catering to their most vile and violent impulses and aspirations," Merkel's Christian Democratic Union/ Christian Social Union (CDU/CSU) coalition has increasingly lost votes to the overtly racist Alternative for Deutschland (AfD) Party.[37]

In August 2015, Merkel declared, "Wir schaffen das" or "We can do this," in regard to Germany taking in refugees, which she asserted was a "national duty."[38] Although by the fall of 2015, her stance on refugees became more restrictive, the AfD's rejection of Merkel's refugee policy attracted former CDU/CSU supporters and gained the AfD seats in three regional March 2016 elections. In September 2017, Merkel gained her fourth term as chancellor, but the AfD won ninety-four seats in the federal parliament, making it the third most powerful party in the country.[39]

It took Merkel months to form a coalition government between her CDU, the CSU, and the Social Democratic Party (SPD) as the CSU and SPD pressured Merkel from opposite positions on refugee policy. Even though the CDU and CSU had been close allies for decades, many conservatives, including CSU leader and Interior Minister, Horst Seehofer, found Merkel's stance on refugees too liberal while the SPD found it too conservative. The coalition almost fell apart in the summer of 2018. To appease the CSU, Merkel agreed to tighten controls at the Austrian border to prevent people from entering Germany if they had already applied for asylum in another EU country. She also pledged to set up "transit centers" to detain these people, but an SPD spokesperson refused to commit to the "transit centers" in an interview with the newspaper, *Die Welt*. The SPD had firmly rejected setting up these "centers" in 2015 when the number of people entering Germany was at its highest.[40]

At the CDU/CSU youth wing's 2018 meeting, many delegates remained pointedly seated as the chancellor entered the hall to give her address. In her speech, Merkel emphasized Germany's strong economy, outlined its infrastructure challenges, and expressed her displeasure that the country had just spent three years arguing over migration. Insisting that her party members refrain from nationalism, Merkel invoked European political history and drew parallels between Germans' conflicts with "migrants" and conflicts between eastern and western Germans:

> What did the founding fathers of Europe mean when they said nationalism will lead to war again? . . . let's not start dividing ourselves into groups again. The migrants and the Germans. Those in

the East and those in the West. The first thing is the stereotypes, secondly come the thoughts being spoken out loud, the language, the hate-speech, and thirdly there are the acts against other groups.[41]

Merkel's critique is suggestive of Gregory Stanton's outline of "classification," "dehumanization," "polarization," and other stages of genocide. Stanton describes how to assess the stages and intervene.[42] Merkel's speech, which also alludes to her personal history, was an intervention on the escalation of stereotypes into violence. Merkel grew up in East Germany, then experienced the unification era's east–west tensions, and the post-unification spike in racist nationalism including violent scapegoating against people seeking political asylum.[43]

As Trump had in his 2017 UN address, in her speech to the youth wing, Merkel rhetorically reached back to "founding fathers," reflecting a male-centered political history. Whereas Trump referred to national founding fathers, Merkel summoned supranational founding fathers. White men are central to both narratives, which reference them as sources of enlightened principles and normative political culture.[44]

Merkel's reference to a European Union origin story reinforces the idea of white cultural superiority even as she passionately speaks against nationalism and prejudice. Regardless of Merkel's intention, alluding to these elite so-called fathers as fonts of advanced political thinking supports the myth that Western civilization has been particularly prolific in producing sophisticated individuals, ideas, documents, and cultures. It also implies that the solutions to Europe's twenty-first-century problems are distinctly European when, in fact, the historic European idea of white cultural superiority is at the root of contemporary nationalism and the anti-refugee scapegoating which Merkel denounces.

As 1945–1959 was the EU's foundational period, the idea of white cultural superiority predates the European Union by centuries. Collaborating in the aftermath of two world wars both started by Europeans, the "founding fathers" intended the EU to prevent war between European nations. Combatting the idea of white cultural superiority was not their priority. Europeans used the myth of white cultural superiority to undergird over 400 years of racist oppression the horrors of which continued into the five decades it took to launch the EU's common currency and borders. During much of the EU's development, codified racist discrimination permeated almost every aspect of people's lives in Europe and European-derived nations.[45]

When communicating to the youth wing of a conservative German political party, references to European "founding fathers" may be more compelling than referring to the United Nations or a nonwhite majority institution although Merkel can partly thank the UN's Decade of Women for her political career. Considering her positionality and the AfD's Euroskepticism, employing the European founders may have been part of a rhetorical strategy just as wearing a pant suit is part of the repertoire of methods that politically powerful European and North American women apply in establishing and maintaining their credibility. Mushaben describes how Merkel's rise to her status as the "World's Most Powerful Woman" and membership in the "elite club" of the "Sisterhood of the Traveling Pantsuits" necessitated a political and physical makeover as well as intentionally gender-neutral campaigning. The first German woman head of state and the first woman leader of her party, Merkel overcame many patriarchal hurdles before her controversial 2015 refugee stance. The hurdles included at least 15 media-planted gendered labels, which started with "Kohl's girl"—a reference to Helmut Kohl who preceded her as chancellor. The mother/mommy/mutti references to Merkel have been the most tenacious although, in the last ten years, they were often not intended as critiques.[46]

The AfD's misogyny has increased as Merkel's political power has decreased. As people of all genders participate in military masculinity and the masculinity ideology of elite U.S. politics, women can contribute to patriarchal gender ideologies and play lead roles in racist nationalism and anti-refugee policies. Until she resigned due to legal issues and the birth of her fifth child, Frauke Petry was the AfD's most recognizable figure. During Petry's co-chairship, the AfD advocated for "'classic family values,'" and Petry advocated for police shooting refugees at the border. Alice Weidel leads the AfD's "'moderate'" faction. She argues that Germany is being Islamified. Regardless that Weidel is in a domestic partnership with another woman with whom she has two children, the AfD's proposed sexual education curriculum teaches that marriage is between a man and a woman.[47]

As in the United States, in Germany, politicians have utilized racist stereotypes in portrayals of refugees as terrorists, sexual predators, and criminals. Lies which rely on a distortion of facts are particularly powerful. Those who want to further restrict Germany's refugee policies have perpetuated stereotypes by citing actual crimes allegedly committed by men with refugee status. Most infamously, on New Year's Eve of 2015–2016, groups of men committed a rash of robberies and sexual assaults, primarily, in Cologne. The Cologne police chief reported that the attackers were men were of "North African or Arab appearance."[48] Whether or not the perpetrators had refugee status, it is pernicious to seize on the criminality of even a large group of men in order to nurture myths about hundreds of thousands, if not, millions of people.

In response to these crimes, Sahra Wagenknecht, the parliamentary chair of The Left (Die Linke) Party, said, "Whoever abuses their guest's rights has also forfeited their guest's rights." This comment sparked controversy within her party as it seemed to suggest that Germany should ignore the Geneva Convention on refugee rights. Wagenknecht rescinded her remark but, then, raised the issue during a discussion on caps for refugee numbers. In March 2016, a German newspaper quoted her saying, "Not all the refugees can come."[49]

While Lipsitz's *The Possessive Investment in Whiteness* is about the United States, it is easy to imagine that white people in Germany and elsewhere would also profit from exploring how whiteness relates to their material, social, and political lives.[50] To what extent are they investing in narrow self-interest or living up to the values which they espouse? In the words of a President who was loathed by liberals, in many circumstances and institutions, they are "the decider[s]."[51] "In the age of Donald Trump," and before it, white liberals and leftists have played essential roles in maintaining white domination and the myth of white cultural superiority.[52] Like Myer and his staff in the 1940s, middle-class and elite white people today who identify as liberal, leftist, or Democrat need to examine their "possessive investment in whiteness" and their roles as gatekeepers and policymakers in the public, nonprofit, and private sectors.

Americans and Germans have much work to do including fundamentally rethinking their national identities and how they operationalize them. U.S. and German political leaders need to find ways to fight terrorism without mangling human rights. Domestic racism and inhumane refugee policies undermine legitimate efforts to combat terrorism. In response to the Muslim ban, Republicans Lindsay Graham and John McCain released a joint statement:

> We fear this executive order will become a self-inflicted wound in the fight against terrorism. [It] sends a signal, intended or not, that America does not want Muslims coming to our country. . . this executive order may do more to help terrorist recruitment than improve our security.[53]

In 2003, Yamamoto, Serrano and Rodriguez wrote:

> . . . the United States will lack unfettered moral authority and international standing to sustain a preemptive worldwide war on

terror unless it fully and fairly redresses the continuing harms of its own historic government-sponsored terrorizing of [African Americans]. . . the United States' international standing will be jeopardized by the government's exercise of. . . power for largely nondefensive political ends in a manner that subverts civil liberties at home and human rights abroad.[54]

Since 2003, Europe has suffered terrorist attacks in Spain, France, and Germany, and Europeans, too, have "subverted" human rights in the name of fighting terrorism. Before Trump's election, twenty-first-century human rights violations such as those at Abu Ghraib and police murders of civilians as well as internationally known historic violations had already tainted the image of the United States.[55] Trump's presidency has further reduced the United States' standing. In this context, international and domestic criticism of racism and the U.S. and German governments' willingness to misuse "national security" are on trial in the global court of public opinion.

While the U.S. and German political leadership continue to portray Europe and European-derived nations as pinnacles of human culture, their antirefugee politics embolden those whose hatred takes violent forms. In Germany, racist violence is increasing and, in 2015, racists committed more than 1,000 attacks on asylum centers. The director of the United States' Southern Poverty Law Center's Intelligence Project has stated that the increase in hate crimes in the United States can be related directly to Trump. These acts of domestic terrorism fuel an international terrorist narrative, which claims that Western racism and imperialism justify terrorism.[56]

During a 2018 European trip, Steve Bannon, Trump's former chief strategist and the architect of the Muslim ban, met with Alice Weidel of the Alternative for Deutschland Party.[57] As racist nationalists build on their commonalities across national boundaries so, too, must those who critique them. Those who identify as part of an opposition to human rights violations, antirefugee policies or institutionalized oppression also need to build on commonalities across identities and national boundaries.

Angela Davis urges people who are struggling against racism to make international linkages. She calls for social movements to "raise parallels and similarities in other parts of the world" by, for example, asking what structural similarities there are between events in Ferguson and those in Palestine.[58] Teaching and learning about these connections and operationalizing them as part of political actions could make for a positive disruption of the status quo.[59]

As a contribution to understanding international parallels, this book connects twentieth-century U.S. policies to twenty-first-century U.S. and Germany policies and demonstrates how the contemporary policies relate to each other.[60] Hopefully, I have also conveyed how the World War II human rights violations of Japanese Americans are connected to policies which targeted European immigrants in the United States, Native Americans, and African Americans. Audre Lorde taught that there are "no single-issue lives."[61] Similarly, there is no credible single-issue policy analysis if one aims to unravel gender, race, and nation, the fundamental tensions of our time.

Notes

1 *Los Angeles Times*, "Read President Trump's Full Remarks at the U.N. General Assembly, Annotated," Sept. 19, 2017, www.latimes.com/world/la-fg-trump-united-nations-address-transcript-20170919-htmlstory.html#.
2 Ben Knight, "Angela Merkel Gets Tough Love from Her Party's Youth Wing," *DW*, Oct. 6, 2018. www.dw.com/en/angela-merkel-gets-tough-love-from-her-partys-youth-wing/a-45780383.
3 *BBC News*, "Europe and Nationalism: A Country-by-Country Guide," Sept. 10, 2018. www.bbc.com/news/world-europe-36130006. Yeganeh Torbati and Omar Mohhamed, "Special Reports: Slamming the Door—How Trump Transformed U.S. Refugee Program," *Reuters*, Sept. 12, 2018, www.reuters.com/article/us-usa-immigration-refugees-specialrepor/special-report-slamming-the-door-how-trump-transformed-u-s-refugee-program-idUSKCN1LS1H8. Wesley Dockery, "Two Years since Germany Opened its Borders to Refugees: A Chronology," *DW*, April 9, 2018, www.dw.com/en/two-years-since-germany-opened-its-borders-to-refugees-a-chronology/a-40327634. Mushaben, 265.
4 Charlotte Edmond, "The Number of Displaced People in the World Just Hit a Record High," *World Economic Forum*, June 20, 2017. UNHCR, "Figures at a Glance," Nov. 19, 2018, www.unhcr.org/en-us/figures-at-a-glance.html. Torbati and Mohhamed. Dockery. *DW*, "AfD: What You Need to Know about Germany's Far-Right Party," Sept. 24, 2017, www.dw.com/en/afd-what-you-need-to-know-about-germanys-far-right-party/a-37208199.
5 Donald Trump, "Transcript: Donald Trump Announces His Presidential Candidacy," *CBS News*, June 16, 2015, www.cbsnews.com/news/transcript-donald-trump-announces-his-presidential-candidacy/.
6 Donald Trump, "Transcript."
7 *BBC News*, "President Trump: 'I Am Totally Opposed to Domestic Violence,'" Feb. 14, 2018, www.bbc.com/news/av/world-us-canada-43066383/president-trump-i-am-totally-opposed-to-domestic-violence. Sandra Park, "Jeff Sessions Slams the Door on Immigrants Desperate to Escape Domestic Violence," ACLU, Aug. 16, 2018, www.aclu.org/blog/immigrants-rights/deportation-and-due-process/jeff-sessions-slams-door-immigrants-desperate. Jessica Winter, "The Language of the Trump Administration Is the Language of Domestic Violence," *New Yorker*, June 11, 2018, www.newyorker.com/culture/cultural-comment/the-language-of-the-trump-administration-is-the-language-of-domestic-violence.

8 Robert D. Dean, *Imperial Brotherhood: Gender and the Making of Cold War Foreign Policy* (Amherst, MA: University of Massachusetts, 2003), 10. Michael D'Antonio, in Michael Kirk, Mike Wiser and Philip Bennett, "The Choice, 2016" Transcript, *PBS*, Accessed Sept. 30, 2018, www.pbs. org/wgbh/frontline/film/the-choice-2016/transcript/.

9 Dean, 4, 5, 6, 169. Kirk, Wiser, and Bennett.

10 Dean, 7, 169–170.

11 Tom Foreman, "The Story behind Donald Trump's Siblings," *CNN*, Sept. 8, 2015. www.cnn.com/videos/politics/2015/09/08/donald-trumps-siblings-foreman-dnt-erin.cnn. Kirk, Wiser, and Bennett.

12 Kirk, Wiser, and Bennett.

13 Ibid. Sandy McIntosh, in Kirk, Wiser and Bennett.

14 Michael D'Antonio and Tony Schwartz, in Kirk, Wiser and Bennett. Kirk, Wiser, and Bennett. Crispin, Sartwell, "All the President's Men and Their Styles of Masculinity; Trump Be the First Man with His Particular Sort of Swagger to Make It to the White House," *Wall Street Journal* (Online), Aug. 4, 2017, http://proxy.lib.csus.edu/login?url=https://search-proquest-com.proxy.lib.csus.edu/docview/1925905705?accountid=10358.

15 Dean, 3.

16 Ronald Takaki, *Hiroshima: Why America Dropped the Atomic Bomb* (Boston, MA: Little, Brown, and Co., 1995), 115. *BBC News*, "Trump to Kim: My Nuclear Button Is 'Bigger and More Powerful,'" Jan. 3, 2018, www.bbc.com/news/world-asia-42549687. Bob Woodward, *Fear: Trump in the White House* (New York: Simon & Schuster, 2018), 262.

17 "Executive Order Protecting the Nation from Foreign Terrorist Entry into the United States," Executive Orders, White House, Jan. 27, 2017, www.whitehouse.gov/presidential-actions/executive-order-protecting-nation-foreign-terrorist-entry-united-states/.

18 Michael Kirk, "Bannon's War," Transcript, *PBS*, Accessed Dec. 3, 2018, www.pbs.org/wgbh/frontline/film/bannons-war/transcript/.

19 Peter Baker, in Kirk.

20 Robert Costa, in Kirk.

21 "JACL Submits Amicus Brief to SCOTUS in Opposition to Muslim Travel Ban," Japanese American Citizens League, Sept. 19, 2017, https://jacl. org/jacl-submits-amicus-brief-to-scotus-in-opposition-to-muslim-travel-ban/. *BBC News*, "Trump Travel Ban: What Does This Ruling Mean?" June 26, 2018, www.bbc.com/news/world-us-canada-39044403.

22 *Los Angeles Times*, "Read."

23 Mythili Sampathkumar, "Nine Members of the UN Human Rights Council Accused of Violating Human Rights," *Independent*, Sept. 21, 2017, www.independent.co.uk/news/world/politics/un-human-rights-council-members-saudi-arabia-china-venezuela-abusers-violators-a7958271.html. Jamil Dakwar, "Trump Administration Threatens International Criminal Court Judges and Prosecutors for Doing Their Jobs," Sept. 11, 2018, www.aclu.org/blog/human-rights/human-rights-and-national-security/trump-administration-threatens-international.

24 Aaron Blake, "6 Takeaways from Trump's '60 Minutes' Interview," *Washington Post*, Oct. 15, 2018 www.washingtonpost.com/politics/2018/10/15/takeaways-trumps-minutes-interview/?utm_term=.0bfcab86439a.

25 Dakwar, "Trump Administration."

26 Salvador Rizzo, "The Facts about Trump's Policy of Separating Families at the Border," *Washington Post*, June 19, 2018, www.washingtonpost. com/news/fact-checker/wp/2018/06/19/the-facts-about-trumps-policy-of-separating-families-at-the-border/?utm_term=.bec08cc1bc94.

27 *BBC News*, "Trump Wades into German Migration Row," June 18, 2018, www.bbc.com/news/world-us-canada-44524873.

28 *BBC News*, "Trump Wades."

29 Michael Scherer and Josh Dawsey, "Trump Cites as a Negotiating Tool His Policy of Separating Immigrant Children from Their Parents," *Washington Post*, June 15, 2018, www.washingtonpost.com/politics/trump-cites-as-a-negotiating-tool-his-policy-of-separating-immigrant-children-from-their-parents/2018/06/15/ade82b80-70b3-11e8-bf86-a2351b5ece99_story. html?utm_term=.ab59c14fd885&wpisrc=nl_most&wpmm=1. Rizzo. Natalie Stechyson, "Canada's Doctors, Parents Despair at U.S. Border Child Separation and Detention," *Huffington Post*, June 21, 2018, www.huffington-post.ca/2018/06/21/us-border-children-detained_a_23464785/. Aaron Belkin, *Bring Me Men: Military Masculinity and the Benign Façade of American Empire, 1898–2001* (New York: Columbia University Press, 2012), 3–4.

30 Anne Gearan, Josh Dawsey, and John Wagner, "Nikki Haley Resigns as Trump's UN Ambassador," *Washington Post*, Oct. 9, 2018, www.washingtonpost. com/politics/trump-says-hell-make-an-announcement-about-nikki-haley-amid-reports-she-is-resigning-as-un-ambassador/2018/10/09/bfd62eee-cbcd-11e8-a360-85875bac0b1f_story.html?noredirect=on&utm_term=. a5a8fc627b01&wpisrc=nl_most&wpmm=1. Rick Gladstone, "U.S. Quits Migration Pact Saying It Infringes on Sovereignty," *New York Times*, Dec. 3, 2017, www.nytimes.com/2017/12/03/world/americas/united-nations-migration-pact.html. Jeff Stein, "The U.N. Says 18.5 Million Americans Are in 'Extreme Poverty.' Trump's Team Says Only 250,000 Are," *Washington Post*, June 25, 2018, www.washingtonpost.com/news/wonk/wp/2018/06/25/ trump-team-rebukes-u-n-saying-it-overestimates-extreme-poverty-in-america-by-18-million-people/?utm_term=.b10f30f265c9.

31 Woodward, 66.

32 Gearan, Dawsey, and Wagner.

33 Henry A. Giroux, "White Nationalism, Armed Culture and State Violence in the Age of Donald Trump," *Philosophy and Social Criticism* 43, no. 9 (2017): 900.

34 *BBC News*, "US Slashes Number of Refugees to 30,000," Sept. 18, 2018, www.bbc.com/news/world-us-canada-45555357. Torbati and Mohhamed. U.S. Secretary of State, Mike Pompeo, stated that the new policy "serves the national security interests."

35 *BBC News*, "Trump Wades."

36 Dockery.

37 Ben Knight, "Berlin Protests against Far-Right Politics Draw Thousands," *DW*, Oct. 13, 2018, www.dw.com/en/berlin-protests-against-far-right-politics-draw-thousands/a-45873439. George Lipsitz, *The Possessive Investment in Whiteness: How White People Profit from Identity Politics* (Philadelphia, PA: Temple University Press, 2018), 260, ProQuest Ebook Central, https:// ebookcentral.proquest.com/lib/csus/detail.action?docID=542533483. *DW*, "Record-low Support for Angela Merkel's Government," Oct. 18, 2018, www. dw.com/en/record-low-support-for-angela-merkels-government/a-45950376.

BBC News, "German Anger over AfD Chief's 'Nazi Era just Bird Poo' Remark," June 4, 2018, www.bbc.com/news/world-europe-44354559.
38 Dockery.
39 *DW*, "AfD." Melissa Eddy, "Alternative for Germany Who Are They and What Do They Want," *New York Times* (online) Sept. 25, 2017, www.nytimes.com/2017/09/25/world/europe/germany-election-afd.html.
40 Dockery. *DW*, "AfD." *BBC News*, "Germany Migrants: Merkel Averts Coalition Government Split," July 3, 2018, www.bbc.com/news/world-europe-44685727. *DW*, "Germany Extends Border Controls with Austria and Denmark," Oct. 12, 2018, *DW*, www.dw.com/en/germany-extends-border-controls-with-austria-and-denmark/a-45868897?maca=en-rss-en-ger-1023-xml-atom. *DW*, "Germany Steps Up Incentives for Refugee Self-Deportation," March 30, 2018, www.dw.com/en/germany-steps-up-incentives-for-refugee-self-deportation/av-43193005. *BBC News*, "Horst Seehofer: Islam Does Not Belong to Germany, Says New Minister," March 16, 2018, www.bbc.com/news/world-europe-43422770. Nicole Goebel, "Migration 'Mother of all Political Problems,' Says German Interior Minister Horst Seehofer," *DW*, Sept. 6, 2018, www.dw.com/en/migration-mother-of-all-political-problems-says-german-interior-minister-horst-seehofer/a-45378092. *BBC News*, "Horst Seehofer: Islam Does Not Belong to Germany, Says New Minister," March 16, 2018, www.bbc.com/news/world-europe-43422770. Nicole Goebel, "Migration 'Mother of all Political Problems,' Says German Interior Minister Horst Seehofer," *DW*, Sept. 6, 2018, www.dw.com/en/migration-mother-of-all-political-problems-says-german-interior-minister-horst-seehofer/a-45378092.
41 *DW*, "Angela."
42 Gregory H. Stanton, "Ten Stages of Genocide," The Genocide Education Project, revised 2013, https://genocideeducation.org/wp-content/uploads/2016/03/ten_stages_of_genocide.pdf.
43 Joyce Marie Mushaben, *Becoming Madam Chancellor: Angela Merkel and the Berlin Republic* (Cambridge: Cambridge University Press, 2017), 73–77, 253, 255.
44 *Los Angeles Times*, "Read." *DW*, "Angela."
45 "The History of the European Union," European Union, last published on Jan. 25, 2019, https://europa.eu/european-union/about-eu/history_en.
46 Sean Clarke, "German Elections 2017: Full Results," *Guardian*, Sept. 24, 2017, www.theguardian.com/world/ng-interactive/2017/sep/24/german-elections-2017-latest-results-live-merkel-bundestag-afd. Mushaben, 1–4, 21–22, 35, 39.
47 Mushaben, 303. *DW*, "AfD: What You Need to Know about Germany's Far-Right Party," Sept. 24, 2017, www.dw.com/en/afd-what-you-need-to-know-about-germanys-far-right-party/a-37208199. *DW*, "AfD Publishes Sex Education Proposal Focusing on 'Classical Family Values,'" Nov. 15, 2016, www.dw.com/en/afd-publishes-sex-education-proposal-focusing-on-classical-family-values/a-36401503.
48 *BBC News*, "Germany Shocked by Cologne New Year Gang Assaults on Women," Jan. 5, 2016, www.bbc.com/news/world-europe-35231046.
49 Ben Knight, "Right-wing AfD Poaching Voters from German Left Part," *DW*, May 26, 2016, www.dw.com/en/right-wing-afd-poaching-voters-from-german-left-party/a-19285067.

50 Lipsitz.

51 *CNN*, "Bush: 'I'm the Decider' on Rumsfeld," April 18, 2006, www.cnn. com/2006/POLITICS/04/18/rumsfeld/.

52 Giroux, 889.

53 *UN News*, "'We Must Fight Terrorism Together' Without Sacrificing Legal and Human Rights, Declares UN Chief,'" June 29, 2018, https://news. un.org/en/story/2018/06/1013592. John McCain and Lindsey Graham, quoted in Woodward, 100.

54 Erik Y. Yamamoto, Susan K. Serrano, and Michelle Natividad Rodriguez, "American Racial Justice on Trial—Again: African American Reparations, Human Rights, and the War on Terror," *Michigan Law Review* 101, no. 5 (March 2003): 1329, doi:10.2307/3595376.

55 Kenneth Baker, "Abu Ghraib's Horrific Images Drove Artist Fernando Botero into Action," *SFGate*, Jan. 29, 2007, www.sfgate.com/author/ kenneth-baker/. Claire Richardson, "Lessons for the US from My Lai, 50 Years after the Massacre," *DW*, March 13, 2018, www.dw.com/en/ lessons-for-the-us-from-my-lai-50-years-after-the-massacre/a-42969338. *DW*, "United States' Global Image Suffering under Donald Trump's Presidency: Survey," June 27, 2018, www.dw.com/en/united-states-global- image-suffering-under-donald-trumps-presidency-survey/a-39431357.

56 Elizabeth Schumacher, "Jewish Student in Berlin Bullied for Months with Anti-Semitic Attacks at Renowned High School," *DW*, June 27, 2018, www.dw.com/en/jewish-student-in-berlin-bullied-for-months-with- anti-semitic-attacks-at-renowned-high-school/a-44430805. Ben Knight, "German Muslims Call for Solidarity over Mosque Attacks," *DW*, March 15, 2018, www.dw.com/en/german-muslims-call-for-solidarity- over-mosque-attacks/a-42994754. Kate Brady, "German City of Cottbus Grapples with Violence between Locals and Refugees," *DW*, Jan. 25, 2018, www.dw.com/en/german-city-of-cottbus-grapples-with-violence- between-locals-and-refugees/a-42309934. Helena Baers, "Germans Increasingly Prejudiced against Foreigners, Muslims," *DW*, Nov. 11, 2018, www.dw.com/en/germans-increasingly-prejudiced-against-foreigners- muslims/a-46180880. Lipsitz, 8, 109, 269. Giroux, 891. Southern Poverty Law Center, "Hate and Extremism in 2018," Southern Poverty Law Center, 2018. *BBC News*, "Trump's Muslim Ban Call 'Endangers US Security,'" Dec. 8, 2015, www.bbc.com/news/world-us-canada-35047105.

57 Elizabeth Schumacher, "Steve Bannon Meets AfD's Alice Weidel during European Far-right Roadshow," *DW*, March 7, 2018, www.dw.com/ en/steve-bannon-meets-afds-alice-weidel-during-european-far-right- roadshow/a-42873730.

58 Angela Y. Davis, *Freedom Is a Constant Struggle: Ferguson, Palestine and the Foundations of a Movement* (Chicago, IL: Hay Market Books, 2016), 77, cited in Giroux, 903.

59 Giroux, 905.

60 Davis.

61 Jamia Wilson, "Young Feminists Care about Multiple Issues," *New York Times*, Aug. 3, 2015, www.nytimes.com/roomfordebate/2015/07/08/ is-hillary-clintons-feminism-out-of-style/young-feminists-care-about- multiple-issues.

References

Primary sources

McWilliams, Carey. Papers. Special Collections. Young Research Library, UCLA, Los Angeles, CA.

Myer, Dillon S. Papers. Personal Correspondence and War Relocation Authority Papers. Truman Library. Independence, MO.

United States War Relocation Authority. Records. Edward Spicer Correspondence. Special Collections. University of Arizona Library, Tucson.

War Relocation Authority. Papers. Headquarters Papers and Correspondence. National Archives. Washington, D.C.

Secondary sources

Anderson, Benedict. *Imagined Communities: Reflections on the Origin and Spread of Nationalism*. London: Verso, 1991.

Anderson, Warwick. *Colonial Pathologies: American Tropical Medicine, Race, and Hygiene in the Philippines*. Durham, NC: Duke University Press, 2006.

Ansel, Adams. *Born Free and Equal: Photographs of Loyal Japanese-Americans in Manzanar Relocation Center, Inyo, California*. New York: U.S. Camera, 1944.

Badger, Tony. "New Deal." In *Encyclopedia of the Great Depression*, Vol. 2, edited by Robert S. McElvaine, 701–711. New York: Macmillan Reference USA, 2004. *Gale Virtual Reference Library*, http://link.galegroup.com/apps/doc/CX3404500395/GVRL?u=csus_main&sid=GVRL&xid=61d8392b.

Baers, Helena. "Germans Increasingly Prejudiced against Foreigners, Muslims." *DW*, Nov. 11, 2018. www.dw.com/en/germans-increasingly-prejudiced-against-foreigners-muslims/a-46180880.

Baker, Kenneth. "Abu Ghraib's Horrific Images Drove Artist Fernando Botero into Action." *SFGate*, Jan. 29, 2007. www.sfgate.com/author/kenneth-baker/.

BBC News. "Trump's Muslim Ban Call 'Endangers US Security.'" Dec. 8, 2015. www.bbc.com/news/world-us-canada-35047105.

———. "Germany Shocked by Cologne New Year Gang Assaults on Women." Jan. 5, 2016. www.bbc.com/news/world-europe-35231046.

———. "Reality Check: The US and Refugees." Jan. 30, 2017. www.bbc.com/news/world-us-canada-38801829.

———. "Trump to Kim: My Nuclear Button Is 'Bigger and More Powerful.'" Jan. 3, 2018. www.bbc.com/news/world-asia-42549687.

———. "President Trump: 'I Am Totally Opposed to Domestic Violence.'" Feb. 14, 2018. www.bbc.com/news/av/world-us-canada-43066383/president-trump-i-am-totally-opposed-to-domestic-violence.

———. "Horst Seehofer: Islam Does Not Belong to Germany, Says New Minister." March 16, 2018. www.bbc.com/news/world-europe-43422770.

———. "German Anger over AfD Chief's 'Nazi Era just Bird Poo' Remark." June 4, 2018. www.bbc.com/news/world-europe-44354559.

———. "Susanna Maria Feldman: Iraqi Murder Suspect Returned to Germany." June 9, 2018. www.bbc.com/news/world-europe-44425783.

———. "Trump at G7: Who's who in Merkel's Photo?" June 10, 2018. www.bbc.com/news/world-us-canada-44426442.

———. "US Asylum: Domestic and Gang Violence Cases 'No Longer Generally Qualify'." June 12, 2018. www.bbc.com/news/world-us-canada-44446923.

———. "Trump Wades into German Migration Row." June 18, 2018. www.bbc.com/news/world-us-canada-44524873.

———. "Trump Travel Ban: What Does This Ruling Mean?" June 26, 2018. www.bbc.com/news/world-us-canada-39044403.

———. "Migrant Crisis: EU Leaders Plan Secure Migrant Centres." June 29, 2018. www.bbc.com/news/world-europe-44652846.

———. "Baby Jesus 'Detained' in US Immigration Protest." July 3, 2018. www.bbc.co.uk/news/world-us-canada-44704580.

———. "Germany Migrants: Merkel Averts Coalition Government Split." July 3, 2018. www.bbc.com/news/world-europe-44685727.

———. "Europe and Nationalism: A Country-by-Country Guide." Sept. 10, 2018. www.bbc.com/news/world-europe-36130006.

———. "Migration to Europe in Charts." Sept. 11, 2018. www.bbc.com/news/world-europe-44660699.

———. "Reality Check: Are Migrants Driving Crime in Germany?" Sept. 13, 2018. www.bbc.com/news/world-europe-45419466.

———. "US Slashes Number of Refugees to 30,000." Sept. 18, 2018. www.bbc.com/news/world-us-canada-45555357.

———. "UN Criticised over New Human Rights Council Members." Oct. 12, 2018. www.bbc.com/news/world-45840980.

———. "Germany Protest: Tens of Thousands March against Far Right." Oct. 13, 2018. www.bbc.com/news/world-europe-45851665.

BBC World Service. "Health Check, Daily Aspirin: Not for Healthy Elderly." Sept. 19, 2018. www.bbc.co.uk/programmes/w3cswjl0.

———. "The Compass, After the Crash." Sept. 29, 2018. www.bbc.co.uk/programmes/w27vql6t.

———. "The Documentary, From Truman to Trump." Nov. 13, 2018. www.bbc.co.uk/programmes/w3csyl4v.

Belkin, Aaron. *Bring Me Men: Military Masculinity and the Benign Façade of American Empire, 1898–2001.* New York: Columbia University Press, 2012.

Bellah, Robert N., Richard Madsen, William M. Sullivan, Ann Swindler, and Steven M. Tipton. *Habits of the Heart: Individualism and Commitment in American Life.* New York: Harper and Row, 1985.

Blake, Aaron. "6 Takeaways from Trump's '60 Minutes' Interview." *The Washington Post*, Oct. 15, 2018. www.washingtonpost.com/politics/2018/10/15/takeaways-trumps-minutes-interview/?utm_term=.0bfcab86439a.

Bottici, Chiara. "Culture Wars." In *The Encyclopedia of Political Science*, Vol. 1, edited by George Thomas Kurian, 370–371. Washington, D.C.: CQ Press, 2011. *Gale Virtual Reference Library*, http://link.galegroup.com/apps/doc/CX1671600329/GVRL?u=csus_main&sid=GVRL&xid=8aed6ea9.

Boyle, Brenda M. *Masculinity in Vietnam War Narratives: A Critical Study of Fiction, Films and Nonfiction Writings.* Jefferson, PA: McFarland & Company, 2009.

Brady, Kate. "German City of Cottbus Grapples with Violence between Locals and Refugees." *DW*, Jan. 25, 2018. www.dw.com/en/german-city-of-cottbus-grapples-with-violence-between-locals-and-refugees/a-42309934.

Brint, Steven. "Higher Education." In *Encyclopedia of Sociology*, Vol. 2, 2nd ed., 1178–1186. New York: Macmillan Reference USA, 2001. *Gale Virtual Reference Library*, http://link.galegroup.com/apps/doc/CX3404400157/GVRLu=csus_main&sid=GVRL&xid=0482197e.

Broady, Maurice. *Planning for People: Essays on the Social Context of Planning.* London: National Council of Social Service, 1968.

Bulman, Robert C. *Hollywood Goes to High School: Cinema, Schools and American Culture.* New York: Worth Publishers, 2015.

Chapman, Roger, ed. "Founding Fathers." In *Culture Wars: An Encyclopedia of Issues, Viewpoints, and Voices*, Vol. 1, 192–193. Armonk: M.E. Sharpe, 2010. *Gale Virtual Reference Library*, http://link.galegroup.com/apps/doc/CX1724100177/GVRL?u=csus_main&sid=GVRL&xid=7bf0cf71.

CNN. "Bush: 'I'm the Decider' on Rumsfeld." April 18, 2006. www.cnn.com/2006/POLITICS/04/18/rumsfeld/.

Connell, Robert W. *Masculinities*, 2nd ed. Berkeley: University of California Press, 2005.

Cosmos Club, Washington D.C. "About the Cosmos Club." Accessed Aug. 22, 2018. www.cosmosclub.org/.

Creef, Elena Tajima. *Imaging Japanese America: The Visual Construction of Citizenship, Nation, and the Body.* New York: New York University Press, 2004.

Clarke, Sean. "German Elections 2017: Full Results." *Guardian*, Sept. 24, 2017. www.theguardian.com/world/ng-interactive/2017/sep/24/german-elections-2017-latest-results-live-merkel-bundestag-afd.

Dakwar, Jamil. "Trump Administration Threatens International Criminal Court Judges and Prosecutors for Doing Their Jobs." ACLU. Sept. 11, 2018.

www.aclu.org/blog/human-rights/human-rights-and-national-security/
trump-administration-threatens-international.

Daniels, Roger. *Concentration Camps, USA: Japanese Americans and World War II*. New York: Holt, Rinehart and Winston, 1971.

———. *The Decision to Relocate the Japanese Americans*. Philadelphia, PA: Lippincott, 1975.

———. "The Forced Migration of West Coast Japanese, 1942–1946: A Quantitative Note." In *Japanese Americans: From Evacuation to Redress*, edited by Roger Daniels, Sandra C. Taylor, and Harry H.L. Kitano, 72–74. Salt Lake City: Utah of University Press, 1986.

Daniels, Roger, Sandra C. Taylor, and Harry H.L. Kitano, eds. *Japanese Americans: From Relocation to Redress*, revised ed. Seattle: University of Washington Press, 1991.

Davis, Angela Y. *Freedom Is a Constant Struggle: Ferguson, Palestine and the Foundations of a Movement*. Chicago, IL: Hay Market Books, 2016.

Dean, Robert D. *Imperial Brotherhood: Gender and the Making of Cold War Foreign Policy*. Amherst, MA: University of Massachusetts Press, 2003.

Department of Justice, Office of Public Affairs. "Attorney General Announces Zero-Tolerance Policy for Criminal Illegal Entry." April 6, 2018. www.justice.gov/opa/pr/attorney-general-announces-zero-tolerance-policy-criminal-illegal-entry.

Dicke, William. "Dillon S. Myer, Who Headed War Relocation Agency, Dies." *The New York Times*, Archives, Oct. 25, 1982. www.nytimes.com/1982/10/25/obituaries/dillon-s-myer-who-headed-war-relocation-agency-dies.html.

Dockery, Wesley. "Two Years Since Germany Opened its Borders to Refugees: A Chronology." *DW*, April 9, 2018. www.dw.com/en/two-years-since-germany-opened-its-borders-to-refugees-a-chronology/a-40327634.

Drinnon, Richard. *Keeper of Concentration Camps: Dillon S. Myer and American Racism*. Berkeley, CA: University of California Press, 1987.

Dudziak, Mary L. "Desegregation as a Cold War Imperative." *Stanford Law Review* 41, no. 1 (1988): 61–120. doi:10.2307/1228836.

Eddy, Melissa. "Alternative for Germany Who Are They and What Do They Want." *New York Times* (online), Sept. 25, 2017. www.nytimes.com/2017/09/25/world/europe/germany-election-afd.html.

Edmond, Charlotte. "The Number of Displaced People in the World Just Hit a Record High." *World Economic Forum*, June 20, 2017.

European Union. "The History of the European Union." Last published on Jan. 25, 2019. https://europa.eu/european-union/about-eu/history_en.

Fahrenthold, David A. "Trump Recorded Having Extremely Lewd Conversation about Women in 2005." *The Washington Post*, Oct. 7, 2016. www.washingtonpost.com/politics/trump-recorded-having-extremely-lewd-conversation-about-women-in-2005/2016/10/07/3b9ce776-8cb4-11e6-bf8a-3d26847eeed4_story.html?utm_term=.973329dd5c2e.

Feinberg, Lawrence. "18 Women End Cosmos Club's 110-Year Male Era." *The Washington Post*, Oct. 12, 1988. www.washingtonpost.com/archive/

local/1988/10/12/18-women-end-cosmos-clubs-110-year-male-era/8cc6e3e1-7562-4435-a607-6b1b6b616f27/?utm_term=.76532283b9ae.

Fenstermaker, Sarah, and Candace West. "'Doing Difference' Revisited: Problems, Prospects, and the Dialogue in Feminist Theory." In *Doing Gender: Doing Difference*, edited by Sarah Fenstermaker and Candace West, 205–216. New York: Routledge, 2002.

Ferguson, Kathy E., and Phyllis Turnbull. *Oh, Say, Can You See? The Semiotics of the Military in Hawai'i*, 155–198. Minneapolis: University of Minnesota Press, 1999.

Foglesong, Richard E. *Planning the Capitalist City: The Colonial Era to the 1920s.* Princeton, NJ: Princeton University Press, 1986.

Foreman, Tom. "The Story behind Donald Trump's Siblings." *CNN*, Sept. 8, 2015. www.cnn.com/videos/politics/2015/09/08/donald-trumps-siblings-foreman-dnt-erin.cnn.

Franklin D. Roosevelt Presidential Library and Museum. "FDR and Japanese American Internment." Accessed Nov. 14, 2018. www.fdrlibrary.marist.edu/archives/pdfs/internment.pdf.

———. "Memorandum to the President from Attorney General Francis Biddle." Accessed Nov. 14, 2018. www.fdrlibrary.marist.edu/archives/pdfs/internment.pdf.

———. J. Edgar Hoover to Edwin M. Watson, "FDR and Japanese American Internment," December 10, 1941. Accessed Nov. 20, 2018. www.fdrlibrary.marist.edu/archives/pdfs/internment.pdf.

Freidel, Frank, and Hugh Sidey. "Dwight D. Eisenhower." "The Presidents of the United States of America." *White House Historical Association.* Accessed Aug. 18, 2018. www.whitehouse.gov/about-the-white-house/presidents/dwight-d-eisenhower/.

———. "Harry S. Truman." "The Presidents of the United States of America." *White House Historical Association.* Accessed Sept. 14, 2018. www.whitehouse.gov/about-the-white-house/presidents/harry-s-truman/.

Friedmann, John. *Planning in the Public Domain: From Knowledge to Action.* Princeton, NJ: Princeton University Press, 1987.

Gearan, Anne, Josh Dawsey, and John Wagner. "Nikki Haley Resigns as Trump's UN Ambassador." *The Washington Post*, Oct. 9, 2018. www.washingtonpost.com/politics/trump-says-hell-make-an-announcement-about-nikki-haley-amid-reports-she-is-resigning-as-un-ambassador/2018/10/09/bfd62eee-cbcd-11e8-a360-85875bac0b1f_story.html?noredirect=on&utm_term=.a5a8fc627b01&wpisrc=nl_most&wpmm=1.

Genzlinger, Neil. "Time Marches . . . Backward!" *The New York Times*, Sept. 3, 2010. www.nytimes.com/2010/09/03/movies/03newsreel.html.

Giroux, Henry A. "White Nationalism, Armed Culture and State Violence in the Age of Donald Trump." *Philosophy and Social Criticism* 43, no. 9 (2017): 887–910.

Gladstone, Rick. "U.S. Quits Migration Pact Saying It Infringes on Sovereignty." *New York Times*, Dec. 3, 2017. www.nytimes.com/2017/12/03/world/americas/united-nations-migration-pact.html.

Goebel, Nicole. "Migration 'Mother of all Political Problems,' Says German Interior Minister Horst Seehofer." *DW*, Sept. 6, 2018. www.dw.com/en/migration-mother-of-all-political-problems-says-german-interior-minister-horst-seehofer/a-45378092.

Grant, Susan-Mary. "Nationalism and Ethnicity: North America." In *Encyclopedia of Race and Racism*, Vol. 3, 2nd ed., edited by Patrick L. Mason, 225–229. Detroit, MI: Macmillan Reference USA, 2013. *Gale Virtual Reference Library*, http://go.galegroup.com/ps/i.do?p=GVRL&u=csus_main&id=GALE%7CCX4190600317&v=2.1&it=r&sid=GVRL&asid=25c792bd.

Grant, Judith, and Peta Tancred. "A Feminist Perspective on State Bureaucracy." In *Gendering Organizational Analysis*, edited by Albert J. Mills and Peta Tancred, 112–128. Newbury Park, CA: Sage Publications, 1992.

Gudridge, Patrick O. "Remember Endo?" *Harvard Law Review* 116, no. 7 (May 2003): 1933–1970.

Hallinan, Maureen T., ed. *Handbook of the Sociology of Education*. New York: Springer, 2006.

Hamedy, Saba, and Joyce Tseng. "All the Times President Trump Has Insulted North Korea." *CNN*, March 9, 2018. www.cnn.com/2017/09/22/politics/donald-trump-north-korea-insults-timeline/index.html.

Hayashi, Brian. *Democratizing the Enemy*. Princeton, NJ: Princeton University Press, 2004.

Hibbard, Michael. "Public Epistemologies and Policy Planning: The Case of American Indian Policy." Ph.D. diss., University of California Los Angeles, 1980.

Hines, Thomas S. *Burnham of Chicago: Architect and Planner*. Chicago, IL: University of Chicago Press, 1974.

Hooper, Barbara. "'Split at the Roots': A Critique of the Philosophical and Political Sources of Modern Planning Doctrine." *Frontiers* 13, no. 1 (1992): 45–79.

Irons, Peter. *Justice at War: The Story of the Japanese Internment Cases*. Berkeley, CA: University of California Press, 1983.

Jacobs, Jane. *The Death and Life of Great American Cities*. New York: Vintage Books, 1992.

Japanese American Citizen League. "JACL Submits Amicus Brief to SCOTUS in Opposition to Muslim Travel Ban." Accessed Dec. 30, 2018. https://jacl.org/jacl-submits-amicus-brief-to-scotus-in-opposition-to-muslim-travel-ban/.

Jarvis, Christina. *The Male Body at War: American Masculinity during World War II*. DeKalb, NC: Northern Illinois University Press, 2004.

Johnson, Allan G. *The Gender Knot: Unraveling Our Patriarchal Legacy*, 3rd ed. Philadelphia, PA: Temple University Press, 2014.

Kang, Jerry. "Denying Prejudice: Internment, Redress, and Denial." *UCLA Law Review* 51 (2004): 933–1013.

———. "Watching the Watchers: Enemy Combatants in the Internment's Shadow." *Law and Contemporary Problems* 68, no. 2 (2005): 255–283. https://scholarship.law.duke.edu/lcp/vol68/iss2/.

Kelly, Lawrence. "Anthropology in the Soil Conservation Service." *Agricultural History* 59, no. 2 (1985): 135–147.

Kimmel, Michael S. *Manhood in America: A Cultural History*, 2nd ed. New York: Oxford University Press, 2006.

Kirk, Michael. "Bannon's War." Transcript, *PBS*, accessed Dec. 3, 2018, www.pbs.org/wgbh/frontline/film/bannons-war/transcript/.

Kirk, Michael, Mike Wiser, and Philip Bennett. "The Choice, 2016" Transcript. *PBS*, 2016. www.pbs.org/wgbh/frontline/film/the-choice-2016/transcript/.

Knight, Ben. "Right-Wing AfD Poaching Voters from German Left Party." *DW*, May 26, 2016. www.dw.com/en/right-wing-afd-poaching-voters-from-german-left-party/a-19285067.

———. "Angela Merkel Gets Tough Love from Her Party's Youth Wing." *DW*, Oct. 6, 2018. www.dw.com/en/angela-merkel-gets-tough-love-from-her-partys-youth-wing/a-45780383.

———. "Berlin Protests against Far-Right Politics Draw Thousands." *DW*, Oct. 13, 2018. www.dw.com/en/berlin-protests-against-far-right-politics-draw-thousands/a-45873439.

———. "Why the Bavarian Election Matters for Angela Merkel." *DW*, Oct. 13, 2018. www.dw.com/en/why-the-bavarian-election-matters-for-angela-merkel/a-45867564.

Koikari, Mire. "'Japanese Eyes, American Heart' Politics of Race, Nation, and Masculinity in Japanese American Veterans' WWII Narratives." *Men and Masculinities* 12, no. 5 (2010): 547–564.

Kramer, Paul A. "The Pragmatic Empire: U.S. Anthropology and Colonial Politics in the Occupied Philippines, 1896–1916." Ph.D. diss., Princeton University, 1998.

———. "Making Concessions: Race and Empire Revisited at the Philippine Exposition, St. Louis, 1901–05." *Radical History Review* 73 (1999): 74–114.

———. *The Blood of Government: Race, Empire, the United States, and the Philippines*. Chapel Hill, NC: University of North Carolina Press, 2006.

Leighton, Alexander H. *The Governing of Men: General Principles and Recommendations Based on Experience at a Japanese Relocation Camp*. Princeton, NJ: Princeton University Press, 1945.

Lind, Andrew. *Hawaii's Japanese: An Experiment with Democracy*. Princeton, NJ: Princeton University Press, 1946.

Lipsitz, George. *The Possessive Investment in Whiteness: How White People Profit from Identity Politics*. Philadelphia, PA: Temple University Press, 2018. ProQuest Ebook Central. https://ebookcentral.proquest.com/lib/csus/detail.action?docID=5425334.

Los Angeles Times. "Read President Trump's Full Remarks at the U.N. General Assembly, Annotated." Sept. 19, 2017. www.latimes.com/world/la-fg-trump-united-nations-address-transcript-20170919-htmlstory.html.

Mangan, J.A., and James Walvin. *Manliness and Morality: Middle-Class Masculinity in Britain and America, 1800–1940*. Manchester: Manchester University Press, 1987.

McIntosh, Peggy. "White Privilege and Male Privilege." In *Race, Class and Gender: An Anthology*, edited by Margaret L. Andersen and Patricia Hill Collins. Belmont, CA: Wadsworth Publishing Company, 1995.

McWilliams, Carey. *Factories in the Field: The Story of Migratory Farm Labor in California*. Boston, MA: Little, Brown & Co., 1939.

———. *Brothers under the Skin*. Boston, MA: Little, Brown & Co., 1943.

———. *Prejudice: Japanese Americans: Symbol of Racial Intolerance*. Boston, MA: Little, Brown & Co., 1944.

———. *Brothers under the Skin*. Boston, MA: Little, Brown & Co., 1964.

———. *Factories in the Field: The Story of Migratory Farm Labor in California*. Berkeley, CA: University of California Press, 1999.

Mills, C. Wright. *The Sociological Imagination*. New York: Oxford University Press, 1959.

Mrozek, Donald J. "The Habit of Victory: the American Military and the Cult of Manliness." In *Manliness and Morality: Middle-Class Masculinity in Britain and America, 1800–1940*. Manchester: Manchester University Press, 1987.

Mushaben, Joyce Marie. *Becoming Madam Chancellor: Angela Merkel and the Berlin Republic*. Cambridge: Cambridge University Press, 2017.

Myer, Dillon S. *An Autobiography of Dillon S. Myer*. Berkeley, CA: University of California, 1970.

———. *Uprooted Americans: The Japanese Americans and the War Relocation Authority during World War II*. Tucson, AZ: University of Arizona Press, 1971.

Masaoka, Kathy. "'Communities Under Siege: Keeping the Faith' Fourth Break the Fast Event." Nikkei for Civil Rights and Redress. Accessed Dec. 30, 2018. www.ncrr-la.org/news/2-8-05/2.html.

Modell, John and Madeline Goodman. "Historical Perspectives." In *At the Threshold: The Developing Adolescent*, edited by S. Shirley Feldman and Glen R. Elliot. Cambridge, MA: Harvard University Press, 1990.

National Archives. "Japanese Relocation during World War II." Page last reviewed on April 10, 2017. www.archives.gov/education/lessons/japanese-relocation.

———. "World War II Enemy Alien Control Program Overview." Page last reviewed on July 12, 2018. www.archives.gov/research/immigration/enemy-aliens-overview.

The New York Times. "Milton S. Eisenhower Dies at 85: Served as Advisor to President." May 3, 1985. www.nytimes.com/1985/05/03/us/milton-s-eisenhower-dies-at-85-served-as-adviser-to-president.html.

Nishimoto, Richard S. *Inside an American Concentration Camp: Japanese American Resistance at Poston, Arizona*, edited by Lane Ryo Hirabayashi. Tucson, AZ: University of Arizona Press, 1995.

Park, Sandra. "Jeff Sessions Slams the Door on Immigrants Desperate to Escape Domestic Violence." *ACLU*, Aug. 16, 2018. www.aclu.org/blog/immigrants-rights/deportation-and-due-process/jeff-sessions-slams-door-immigrants-desperate.

Pew Research Center's Social & Demographic Trends. "Top 10 U.S. Metropolitan Areas by Japanese Population, 2015." Japanese in the U.S. Fact Sheet. Sept. 8, 2017. www.pewsocialtrends.org/fact-sheet/asian-americans-japanese-in-the-u-s/.

Pleck, Joseph H. *The Myth of Masculinity*. Cambridge, MA: MIT Press, 1981.

Radzilowski, John. "Hajiro, Barney F." In *Asian and Pacific Islander Americans*, edited by Gary Y. Okihiro, 246–247. Great Lives from History. Vol. 1. Ipswich, MA: Salem Press, 2013. *Gale Virtual Reference Library*, http://link.galegroup.com/apps/doc/CX2075200146/GVRL?u=csus_main&sid=GVRL&xid=a20d192f.

Richardson, Claire. "Lessons for the US from My Lai, 50 Years after the Massacre." *DW*, March 13, 2018. www.dw.com/en/lessons-for-the-us-from-my-lai-50-years-after-the-massacre/a-42969338.

Rizzo, Salvador. "The Facts about Trump's Policy of Separating Families at the Border." *The Washington Post*, June 19, 2018. www.washingtonpost.com/news/fact-checker/wp/2018/06/19/the-facts-about-trumps-policy-of-separating-families-at-the-border/?utm_term=.bec08cc1bc94.

Robinson, Greg. *By Order of the President: FDR and the Internment of Japanese Americans*. Cambridge, MA: Harvard University Press, 2001.

Robinson, Greg, Jerry Kang, and Hiroshi Motomura. "A Symposium on Greg Robinson's A Tragedy of Democracy: Japanese Confinement in North America." *Asian Pacific American Law Journal* 15, no. 1 (June 2010): 6–29.

Rotundo, Anthony E. *American Manhood: Transformations in Masculinity from the Revolution to the Modern Era*. New York: Basic Books, 1993.

Said, Edward W. *Orientalism*, 1st ed. New York: Pantheon Books, 1978.

Sampathkumar, Mythili. "Nine Members of the UN Human Rights Council Accused of Violating Human Rights," *Independent*, Sept. 21, 2017. www.independent.co.uk/news/world/politics/un-human-rights-council-members-saudi-arabia-china-venezuela-abusers-violators-a7958271.html.

Sartwell, Crispin. "All the President's Men and Their Styles of Masculinity; Trump Be the First Man with His Particular Sort of Swagger to Make It to the White House." *Wall Street Journal* (Online), Aug. 4, 2017. http://proxy.lib.csus.edu/login?url=https://search-proquest-com.proxy.lib.csus.edu/docview/1925905705?accountid=10358.

Saxton, Alexander. 1990. *The Rise and Fall of the White Republic: Class Politics and Mass Culture in Nineteenth-century America*. London: Verso.

Scherer, Michael, and Josh Dawsey. "Trump Cites as a Negotiating Tool His Policy of Separating Immigrant Children from Their Parents." *The Washington Post*, June 15, 2018. www.washingtonpost.com/politics/trump-cites-as-a-negotiating-tool-his-policy-of-separating-immigrant-children-from-their-parents/2018/06/15/ade82b80-70b3-11e8-bf86-a2351b5ece99_story.html?utm_term=.ab59c14fd885&wpisrc=nl_most&wpmm=1.

Schumacher, Elizabeth. "Steve Bannon meets AfD's Alice Weidel during European Far-right Roadshow." *DW*, March 7, 2018. www.dw.com/en/steve-bannon-meets-afds-alice-weidel-during-european-far-right-roadshow/a-42873730.

———. "Jewish Student in Berlin Bullied for Months with Anti-Semitic Attacks at Renowned High School." *DW*, June 27, 2018. www.dw.com/en/

jewish-student-in-berlin-bullied-for-months-with-anti-semitic-attacks-at-renowned-high-school/a-44430805.

Scott, Mel. *American City Planning since 1890.* Berkeley: University of California Press, 1969.

Scott, Joan W. "Gender: A Useful Category of Historical Analysis." *The American Historical Review* 91, no. 5 (1986): 1053–1075.

Sitkoff, Harvey. *A New Deal for Blacks: The Emergence of Civil Rights as a National Issue.* New York: Oxford University Press, 1978.

Smith, J.Y. "Rexford Tugwell, Adviser in FDR's 'Brains Trust,' Dies," *The Washington Post,* July 25, 1979. www.washingtonpost.com/archive/local/1979/07/25/rexford-tugwell-adviser-in-fdrs-brains-trust-dies/68a9b1c6-d8c3-44f7-b7d0-2599bada50c4/?noredirect=on&utm_term=.fd423246b388.

Smith, Geoffrey S. "Nativism." In *Encyclopedia of American Foreign Policy,* Vol. 2, 2nd ed., edited by Richard Dean Burns, Alexander DeConde, and Fredrik Logevall, 511–527. New York: Charles Scribner's Sons, 2002. *Gale Virtual Reference Library,* http://go.galegroup.com/ps/i.do?p=GVRL&u=csus_main&id=GALE%7CCX3402300093&v=2.1&it=r&sid=GVRL&asid=a597a74c.

Southern Poverty Law Center. "Hate and Extremism in 2018." Southern Poverty Law Center, Montgomery, AL, 2018.

Stanton, Gregory H. "Ten Stages of Genocide." Revised 2013. The Genocide Education Project. https://genocideeducation.org/wp-content/uploads/2016/03/ten_stages_of_genocide.pdf.

Starn, Orin. "Engineering Internment: Anthropologists and the War Relocation Authority." *American Ethnologist* 13, no. 4 (1986): 700–720.

Stechyson, Natalie. "Canada's Doctors, Parents Despair at U.S. Border Child Separation and Detention." *Huffington Post,* June 21, 2018. www.huffingtonpost.ca/2018/06/21/us-border-children-detained_a_23464785/

Stein, Jeff. "The U.N. Says 18.5 Million Americans Are in 'Extreme Poverty.' Trump's Team Says Only 250,000 Are." *Washington Post,* June 25, 2018. www.washingtonpost.com/news/wonk/wp/2018/06/25/trump-team-rebukes-u-n-saying-it-overestimates-extreme-poverty-in-america-by-18-million-people/?utm_term=.b10f30f265c9.

Stepto, Gabriel, ed. "The Ongoing Effort for Inclusion in the Military." In *The African-American Years: Chronologies of American History and Experience,* 294–311. New York: Charles Scribner's Sons, 2003. *Gale Virtual Reference Library,* http://link.galegroup.com/apps/doc/CX3409100025/GVRL?u=csus_main&sid=GVRL&xid=a09f10bf.

Stimson Center, The. "About Henry L. Stimson." Accessed Sept. 3, 2018. www.stimson.org/content/about-henry-l-stimson.

Suzik, Jeffrey Ryan. "'Building Better Men' The CCC Boy and the Changing Social Ideals of Manliness." *Men and Masculinities* 2, no. 2 (1999): 152–179.

Takaki, Ronald T. *Hiroshima: Why America Dropped the Atomic Bomb.* Boston, MA: Little, Brown, and Co., 1995.

———. *Iron Cages: Race and Culture in Nineteenth-Century America,* 1st ed. New York: Alfred A. Knopf, 1979.

————. *Double Victory: A Multicultural History of America in World War II.* Boston, MA: Little, Brown and Co., 2000.

————. *A Different Mirror: A History of Multicultural America.* New York: Back Bay Books, 2008.

Tanaka, Michiko, and Akemi Kikumura-Yano. *Through Harsh Winters: The Life of a Japanese Immigrant Woman.* Novato, CA: Chandler & Sharp, 1981.

Thangaraj, Stanley I. *Desi Hoop Dreams: Pickup Basketball and the Making of Asian American Masculinity.* New York: New York University Press, 2015.

Theobald, Paul, and Brianna Theobald. "Education in a Rural Context." In *The Routledge History of Rural America*, edited by Pamela Riney-Kehrberg, 165–179. New York: Routledge, 2016.

Thomas, Dorothy Swaine, Charles Kikuchi, and James Minoru Sakoda. *The Salvage.* Berkeley, CA: University of California Press, 1952.

Torbati, Yeganeh, and Omar Mohhamed. "Special Reports: Slamming the Door-How Trump Transformed U.S. Refugee Program." *Reuters*, Sept. 12, 2018. www.reuters.com/article/us-usa-immigration-refugees-specialrepor/special-report-slamming-the-door-how-trump-transformed-u-s-refugee-program-idUSKCN1LS1H8.

Trump, Donald. "Transcript: Donald Trump Announces His Presidential Candidacy." *CBS News*, June 16, 2015. www.cbsnews.com/news/transcript-donald-trump-announces-his-presidential-candidacy/.

Tugwell, Rexford G. *The Place of Planning in Society: Seven Lectures on the Place of Planning in Society with Special Reference to Puerto Rico.* San Juan: Puerto Rico Planning Board, 1954.

————. *Off Course: From Truman to Nixon.* New York: Praeger, 1971.

————. *Tugwell's Thoughts on Planning*, edited by Salvado M.G. Padilla. Puerto Rico: University of Puerto Rico Press, 1975.

UNESCO. "Asylum Seeker," International Migration Glossary, 2017. "http://www.unesco.org/new/" www.unesco.org/new/en/social-and-human-sciences/themes/international-migration/glossary/ asylum-seeker/.

————. "Refugee," International Migration Glossary, 2017. "http://www.unesco.org/new/en/social-and-human-sciences/" www.unesco.org/new/en/social-and-human-sciences/themes/international-migration/glossary/refugee.

UN News. "'We Must Fight Terrorism Together' Without Sacrificing Legal and Human Rights, Declares UN Chief.'" June 29, 2018. https://news.un.org/en/story/2018/06/1013592.

————. "EU Migration Deal Welcomed by UN Agencies." June 29, 2018. https://news.un.org/en/story/2018/06/1013502.

————. "US Migrant Children Policy Reversal, Still 'Fails' Thousands of Detained Youngsters: UN Rights Experts." June 22, 2018. https://news.un.org/en/story/2018/06/1012832.

UNHCR. "A Guide to International Refugee Protection and Building State Asylum Systems." 2017. www.unhcr.org/en-us/publications/legal/3d4aba564/refugee-protection-guide-international-refugee-law-handbook-parliamentarians.html?query=refugee%20law.

———. "Figures at a Glance." Nov. 19, 2018. www.unhcr.org/en-us/figures-at-a-glance.html.

United Nations. "History of the Document." Accessed Nov. 21, 2018. www.un.org/en/sections/universal-declaration/history-document/index.html.

United States Department of Education. "Table 303.70." Digest of Institute of Education Statistics, Feb. 2017. https://nces.ed.gov/programs/digest/d16/tables/dt16_303.70.asp.

United States Holocaust Memorial Museum. "The Nuremberg Trials." Holocaust Encyclopedia. Accessed Nov. 21, 2018. https://encyclopedia.ushmm.org/content/en/article/the-nuremberg-trials.

———. "Origin of the Term 'Genocide.'" Accessed Oct. 10, 2016. www.ushmm.org/confront-genocide/defining-genocide.

United States War Relocation Authority. *The Relocation Program.* Washington, D.C.: U.S. Government Printing Office, 1946.

———. *WRA: A Story of Human Conservation.* Washington, D.C.: U.S. Government Printing Office, 1946.

Van Dijk, Teun. *Discourse Studies.* London: Sage, 1997.

Vergin, Julia. "Open Day at the Mosque: 'Everyone Must Contribute.'" *DW,* April 10, 2018. Accessed Oct. 5, 2018. www.dw.com/en/open-day-at-the-mosque-everyone-must-contribute/a-45746452.

Verinakis, Theofanis. "The Exception to the Rule." *Social Identities* 13, no. 1 (Jan. 2007): 97–118. doi:10.1080/13504630601163403.

Vevier, Charles. "Yellow Peril." In *Dictionary of American History,* Vol. 8, 3rd ed., edited by Stanley I. Kutler, 577–578. New York: Charles Scribner's Sons, 2003. *Gale Virtual Reference Library,* link.galegroup.com/apps/doc/CX3401804636/GVRL?u=csus_main&sid=GVRL&xid=0fd39965.

Walker, Robert A. *The Planning Function in Urban Government.* Chicago, IL: University of Chicago Press, 1950.

Wallinger, Michael John. "Dispersal of the Japanese American: Rhetorical Strategies of the War Relocation Authority, 1942–1945." Ph.D. diss., University of Oregon, 1975.

Walvin, James. "Symbols of Moral Superiority: Slavery, Sport and the Changing World Order, 1800–1950." In *Manliness and Morality: Middle-Class Masculinity in Britain and America, 1800–1940,* edited by J.A. Mangan and James Walvin, 242–260. Manchester: Manchester University Press, 1987.

Watt, Nicholas. "Brexit: UK Gives up on Hope of Merkel's Help." *BBC,* Oct. 1, 2018. www.bbc.com/news/uk-45706399.

Weglyn, Michi. *Years of Infamy: The Untold Story of America's Concentration Camps.* New York: William Morrow and Co., 1976.

West, Candace, and Don H. Zimmerman. "Doing Gender." *Gender & Society* 1, no. 2 (1987): 125–151.

———. "Accounting for Doing Gender." *Gender & Society* 23, no. 1 (Feb. 2009): 112–122.

The White House. "Executive Order Protecting the Nation from Foreign Terrorist Entry into the United States." Jan. 27, 2017. www.whitehouse.gov/presidential-actions/executive-order-protecting-nation-foreign-terrorist-entry-united-states/.

Wike, Richard, Bruce Stokes, Jacob Poushter, and Janell Fetterolf. "U.S. Image Suffers as Publics around World Question Trump's Leadership." *Pew Research Center*, June 26, 2017. www.pewglobal.org/2017/06/26/u-s-image-suffers-as-publics-around-world-question-trumps-leadership/?utm_content=bufferd6498&utm_medium=social&utm_source=twitter.com&utm_campaign=buffer.

Wilson, Jamia. "Young Feminists Care about Multiple Issues." *The New York Times*, Aug. 3, 2015. www.nytimes.com/roomfordebate/2015/07/08/is-hillary-clintons-feminism-out-of-style/young-feminists-care-about-multiple-issues.

Winter, Jessica. "The Language of the Trump Administration Is the Language of Domestic Violence." *The New Yorker*, June 11, 2018. www.newyorker.com/culture/cultural-comment/the-language-of-the-trump-administration-is-the-language-of-domestic-violence.

Woodward, Bob. *Fear: Trump in the White House.* New York: Simon & Schuster, 2018.

Yamamoto, Eric K. "Beyond Redress: Japanese Americans' Unfinished Business." *Asian Law Journal* 7 (Jan. 2000): 131–138. https://doi.org/10.15779/Z38KW15.

Yamamoto, Eric K., Susan K. Serrano, and Michelle Natividad Rodriguez. "American Racial Justice on Trial – Again: African American Reparations, Human Rights, and the War on Terror." *Michigan Law Review* 101, no. 5 (March 2003): 1269–1337. doi:10.2307/3595376.

Yu, Henry. "Thinking about Orientals: Modernity, Social Science, and Asians in Twentieth-Century America." Ph.D. diss., Princeton University, 1995.

———. *Thinking Orientals: Migration, Contact, and Exoticism in Modern America.* New York: Oxford University Press, 2001.

Index